D1519105

DAVID
LLOYD GEORGE

DAVID LLOYD GEORGE

Deirdre Shearman

CHELSEA HOUSE PUBLISHERS
NEW YORK
PHILADELPHIA

EDITOR-IN-CHIEF: Nancy Toff
EXECUTIVE EDITOR: Remmel T. Nunn
MANAGING EDITOR: Karyn Gullen Browne
COPY CHIEF: Juliann Barbato
ART DIRECTOR: Giannella Garrett
PICTURE EDITOR: Adrian G. Allen
MANUFACTURING MANAGER: Gerald Levine

Staff for DAVID LLOYD GEORGE:

SENIOR EDITOR: John W. Selfridge
ASSISTANT EDITORS: Pierre Hauser, Kathleen McDermott, Bert Yaeger
EDITORIAL ASSISTANT: James Guiry
COPY EDITORS: Gillian Bucky, Sean Dolan, Ellen Scordato, Michael Goodman
ASSISTANT DESIGNER: Jill Goldreyer
PICTURE RESEARCH: Alan Gottlieb
SENIOR DESIGNER: David Murray
PRODUCTION COORDINATOR: Laura McCormick
COVER ILLUSTRATION: Richard Martin

CREATIVE DIRECTOR: Harold Steinberg

Frontispiece courtesy of THE BETTMANN ARCHIVE

3 5 7 9 8 6 4 2

Library of Congress Cataloging in Publication Data

Shearman, Deirdre. DAVID LLOYD GEORGE

(World leaders past & present)
Bibliography: p.
Includes index.
1. Lloyd George, David, 1863–1945—Juvenile literature.
2. Prime ministers—Great Britain—Biography—Juvenile
literature. 3. Great Britain—Politics and government—
1901–1936—Juvenile literature. 4. Great Britain—Politics
and government—1936–1945—Juvenile literature. [1. Lloyd
George, David, 1863–1945. 2. Prime ministers. 3. Great
Britain—History—20th century] I. Title. II. Series.
DA566.9.L5S35   1987   941.082′092′4 [B] [92] 85-19045

ISBN 0-87754-581-2
      0-7910-0650-6 (pbk.)

Contents

JOHN ADAMS
JOHN QUINCY ADAMS
KONRAD ADENAUER
ALEXANDER THE GREAT
SALVADOR ALLENDE
MARC ANTONY
CORAZON AQUINO
YASIR ARAFAT
KING ARTHUR
HAFEZ AL-ASSAD
KEMAL ATATÜRK
ATTILA
CLEMENT ATTLEE
AUGUSTUS CAESAR
MENACHEM BEGIN
DAVID BEN-GURION
OTTO VON BISMARCK
LÉON BLUM
SIMON BOLÍVAR
CESARE BORGIA
WILLY BRANDT
LEONID BREZHNEV
JULIUS CAESAR
JOHN CALVIN
JIMMY CARTER
FIDEL CASTRO
CATHERINE THE GREAT
CHARLEMAGNE
CHIANG KAI-SHEK
WINSTON CHURCHILL
GEORGES CLEMENCEAU
CLEOPATRA
CONSTANTINE THE GREAT
HERNÁN CORTÉS
OLIVER CROMWELL
GEORGES-JACQUES
  DANTON
JEFFERSON DAVIS
MOSHE DAYAN
CHARLES DE GAULLE
EAMON DE VALERA
EUGENE DEBS
DENG XIAOPING
BENJAMIN DISRAELI
ALEXANDER DUBČEK
FRANÇOIS & JEAN-CLAUDE
  DUVALIER
DWIGHT EISENHOWER
ELEANOR OF AQUITAINE
ELIZABETH I
FAISAL
FERDINAND & ISABELLA
FRANCISCO FRANCO
BENJAMIN FRANKLIN

FREDERICK THE GREAT
INDIRA GANDHI
MOHANDAS GANDHI
GIUSEPPE GARIBALDI
AMIN & BASHIR GEMAYEL
GENGHIS KHAN
WILLIAM GLADSTONE
MIKHAIL GORBACHEV
ULYSSES S. GRANT
ERNESTO "CHE" GUEVARA
TENZIN GYATSO
ALEXANDER HAMILTON
DAG HAMMARSKJÖLD
HENRY VIII
HENRY OF NAVARRE
PAUL VON HINDENBURG
HIROHITO
ADOLF HITLER
HO CHI MINH
KING HUSSEIN
IVAN THE TERRIBLE
ANDREW JACKSON
JAMES I
WOJCIECH JARUZELSKI
THOMAS JEFFERSON
JOAN OF ARC
POPE JOHN XXIII
POPE JOHN PAUL II
LYNDON JOHNSON
BENITO JUÁREZ
JOHN KENNEDY
ROBERT KENNEDY
JOMO KENYATTA
AYATOLLAH KHOMEINI
NIKITA KHRUSHCHEV
KIM IL SUNG
MARTIN LUTHER KING, JR.
HENRY KISSINGER
KUBLAI KHAN
LAFAYETTE
ROBERT E. LEE
VLADIMIR LENIN
ABRAHAM LINCOLN
DAVID LLOYD GEORGE
LOUIS XIV
MARTIN LUTHER
JUDAS MACCABEUS
JAMES MADISON
NELSON & WINNIE
  MANDELA
MAO ZEDONG
FERDINAND MARCOS
GEORGE MARSHALL

MARY, QUEEN OF SCOTS
TOMÁŠ MASARYK
GOLDA MEIR
KLEMENS VON METTERNICH
JAMES MONROE
HOSNI MUBARAK
ROBERT MUGABE
BENITO MUSSOLINI
NAPOLÉON BONAPARTE
GAMAL ABDEL NASSER
JAWAHARLAL NEHRU
NERO
NICHOLAS II
RICHARD NIXON
KWAME NKRUMAH
DANIEL ORTEGA
MOHAMMED REZA PAHLAVI
THOMAS PAINE
CHARLES STEWART
  PARNELL
PERICLES
JUAN PERÓN
PETER THE GREAT
POL POT
MUAMMAR EL-QADDAFI
RONALD REAGAN
CARDINAL RICHELIEU
MAXIMILIEN ROBESPIERRE
ELEANOR ROOSEVELT
FRANKLIN ROOSEVELT
THEODORE ROOSEVELT
ANWAR SADAT
HAILE SELASSIE
PRINCE SIHANOUK
JAN SMUTS
JOSEPH STALIN
SUKARNO
SUN YAT-SEN
TAMERLANE
MOTHER TERESA
MARGARET THATCHER
JOSIP BROZ TITO
TOUSSAINT L'OUVERTURE
LEON TROTSKY
PIERRE TRUDEAU
HARRY TRUMAN
QUEEN VICTORIA
LECH WALESA
GEORGE WASHINGTON
CHAIM WEIZMANN
WOODROW WILSON
XERXES
EMILIANO ZAPATA
ZHOU ENLAI

CHELSEA HOUSE PUBLISHERS

ON LEADERSHIP
Arthur M. Schlesinger, jr.

LEADERSHIP, it may be said, is really what makes the world go round. Love no doubt smooths the passage; but love is a private transaction between consenting adults. Leadership is a public transaction with history. The idea of leadership affirms the capacity of individuals to move, inspire, and mobilize masses of people so that they act together in pursuit of an end. Sometimes leadership serves good purposes, sometimes bad; but whether the end is benign or evil, great leaders are those men and women who leave their personal stamp on history.

Now, the very concept of leadership implies the proposition that individuals can make a difference. This proposition has never been universally accepted. From classical times to the present day, eminent thinkers have regarded individuals as no more than the agents and pawns of larger forces, whether the gods and goddesses of the ancient world or, in the modern era, race, class, nation, the dialectic, the will of the people, the spirit of the times, history itself. Against such forces, the individual dwindles into insignificance.

So contends the thesis of historical determinism. Tolstoy's great novel *War and Peace* offers a famous statement of the case. Why, Tolstoy asked, did millions of men in the Napoleonic wars, denying their human feelings and their common sense, move back and forth across Europe slaughtering their fellows? "The war," Tolstoy answered, "was bound to happen simply because it was bound to happen." All prior history predetermined it. As for leaders, they, Tolstoy said, "are but the labels that serve to give a name to an end and, like labels, they have the least possible connection with the event." The greater the leader, "the more conspicuous the inevitability and the predestination of every act he commits." The leader, said Tolstoy, is "the slave of history."

Determinism takes many forms. Marxism is the determinism of class. Nazism the determinism of race. But the idea of men and women as the slaves of history runs athwart the deepest human instincts. Rigid determinism abolishes the idea of human freedom—

the assumption of free choice that underlies every move we make, every word we speak, every thought we think. It abolishes the idea of human responsibility, since it is manifestly unfair to reward or punish people for actions that are by definition beyond their control. No one can live consistently by any deterministic creed. The Marxist states prove this themselves by their extreme susceptibility to the cult of leadership.

More than that, history refutes the idea that individuals make no difference. In December 1931 a British politician crossing Park Avenue in New York City between 76th and 77th Streets around 10:30 P.M. looked in the wrong direction and was knocked down by an automobile—a moment, he later recalled, of a man aghast, a world aglare: "I do not understand why I was not broken like an eggshell or squashed like a gooseberry." Fourteen months later an American politician, sitting in an open car in Miami, Florida, was fired on by an assassin; the man beside him was hit. Those who believe that individuals make no difference to history might well ponder whether the next two decades would have been the same had Mario Constasino's car killed Winston Churchill in 1931 and Giuseppe Zangara's bullet killed Franklin Roosevelt in 1933. Suppose, in addition, that Adolf Hitler had been killed in the street fighting during the Munich *Putsch* of 1923 and that Lenin had died of typhus during World War I. What would the 20th century be like now?

For better or for worse, individuals do make a difference. "The notion that a people can run itself and its affairs anonymously," wrote the philosopher William James, "is now well known to be the silliest of absurdities. Mankind does nothing save through initiatives on the part of inventors, great or small, and imitation by the rest of us—these are the sole factors in human progress. Individuals of genius show the way, and set the patterns, which common people then adopt and follow."

Leadership, James suggests, means leadership in thought as well as in action. In the long run, leaders in thought may well make the greater difference to the world. But, as Woodrow Wilson once said, "Those only are leaders of men, in the general eye, who lead in action. . . . It is at their hands that new thought gets its translation into the crude language of deeds." Leaders in thought often invent in solitude and obscurity, leaving to later generations the tasks of imitation. Leaders in action—the leaders portrayed in this series—have to be effective in their own time.

And they cannot be effective by themselves. They must act in response to the rhythms of their age. Their genius must be adapted, in a phrase of William James's, "to the receptivities of the moment." Leaders are useless without followers. "There goes the mob," said the French politician hearing a clamor in the streets. "I am their leader. I must follow them." Great leaders turn the inchoate emotions of the mob to purposes of their own. They seize on the opportunities of their time, the hopes, fears, frustrations, crises, potentialities. They succeed when events have prepared the way for them, when the community is awaiting to be aroused, when they can provide the clarifying and organizing ideas. Leadership ignites the circuit between the individual and the mass and thereby alters history.

It may alter history for better or for worse. Leaders have been responsible for the most extravagant follies and most monstrous crimes that have beset suffering humanity. They have also been vital in such gains as humanity has made in individual freedom, religious and racial tolerance, social justice and respect for human rights.

There is no sure way to tell in advance who is going to lead for good and who for evil. But a glance at the gallery of men and women in *World Leaders—Past and Present* suggests some useful tests.

One test is this: do leaders lead by force or by persuasion? By command or by consent? Through most of history leadership was exercised by the divine right of authority. The duty of followers was to defer and to obey. "Theirs not to reason why,/ Theirs but to do and die." On occasion, as with the so-called "enlightened despots" of the 18th century in Europe, absolutist leadership was animated by humane purposes. More often, absolutism nourished the passion for domination, land, gold and conquest and resulted in tyranny.

The great revolution of modern times has been the revolution of equality. The idea that all people should be equal in their legal condition has undermined the old structure of authority, hierarchy and deference. The revolution of equality has had two contrary effects on the nature of leadership. For equality, as Alexis de Tocqueville pointed out in his great study *Democracy in America*, might mean equality in servitude as well as equality in freedom.

"I know of only two methods of establishing equality in the political world," Tocqueville wrote. "Rights must be given to every citizen, or none at all to anyone . . . save one, who is the master of all." There was no middle ground "between the sovereignty of all and the absolute power of one man." In his astonishing prediction of 20th-century totalitarian dictatorship, Tocqueville explained how the revolution of equality could lead to the *"Führerprinzip"* and more terrible absolutism than the world had ever known.

But when rights are given to every citizen and the sovereignty of all is established, the problem of leadership takes a new form, becomes more exacting than ever before. It is easy to issue commands and enforce them by the rope and the stake, the concentration camp and the *gulag.* It is much harder to use argument and achievement to overcome opposition and win consent. The Founding Fathers of the United States understood the difficulty. They believed that history had given them the opportunity to decide, as Alexander Hamilton wrote in the first Federalist Paper, whether men are indeed capable of basing government on "reflection and choice, or whether they are forever destined to depend . . . on accident and force."

Government by reflection and choice called for a new style of leadership and a new quality of followership. It required leaders to be responsive to popular concerns, and it required followers to be active and informed participants in the process. Democracy does not eliminate emotion from politics; sometimes it fosters demagoguery; but it is confident that, as the greatest of democratic leaders put it, you cannot fool all of the people all of the time. It measures leadership by results and retires those who overreach or falter or fail.

It is true that in the long run despots are measured by results too. But they can postpone the day of judgment, sometimes indefinitely, and in the meantime they can do infinite harm. It is also true that democracy is no guarantee of virtue and intelligence in government, for the voice of the people is not necessarily the voice of God. But democracy, by assuring the right of opposition, offers built-in resistance to the evils inherent in absolutism. As the theologian Reinhold Niebuhr summed it up, "Man's capacity for justice makes democracy possible, but man's inclination to injustice makes democracy necessary."

A second test for leadership is the end for which power is sought. When leaders have as their goal the supremacy of a master race or the promotion of totalitarian revolution or the acquisition and exploitation of colonies or the protection of greed and privilege or the preservation of personal power, it is likely that their leadership will do little to advance the cause of humanity. When their goal is the abolition of slavery, the liberation of women, the enlargement of opportunity for the poor and powerless, the extension of equal rights to racial minorities, the defense of the freedoms of expression and opposition, it is likely that their leadership will increase the sum of human liberty and welfare.

Leaders have done great harm to the world. They have also conferred great benefits. You will find both sorts in this series. Even "good" leaders must be regarded with a certain wariness. Leaders are not demigods; they put on their trousers one leg after another just like ordinary mortals. No leader is infallible, and every leader needs to be reminded of this at regular intervals. Irreverence irritates leaders but is their salvation. Unquestioning submission corrupts leaders and demands followers. Making a cult of a leader is always a mistake. Fortunately hero worship generates its own antidote. "Every hero," said Emerson, "becomes a bore at last."

The signal benefit the great leaders confer is to embolden the rest of us to live according to our own best selves, to be active, insistent, and resolute in affirming our own sense of things. For great leaders attest to the reality of human freedom against the supposed inevitabilities of history. And they attest to the wisdom and power that may lie within the most unlikely of us, which is why Abraham Lincoln remains the supreme example of great leadership. A great leader, said Emerson, exhibits new possibilities to all humanity. "We feed on genius. . . . Great men exist that there may be greater men."

Great leaders, in short, justify themselves by emancipating and empowering their followers. So humanity struggles to master its destiny, remembering with Alexis de Tocqueville: "It is true that around every man a fatal circle is traced beyond which he cannot pass; but within the wide verge of that circle he is powerful and free; as it is with man, so with communities."

1

A Boyhood in Wales

April 17, 1890, was budget day in the House of Commons, the day on which the government's finance minister presents his new budget. The benches on both sides of the Commons were densely packed. It was also the day on which a new member was to be introduced.

Usually when new members are introduced to the Commons, they arrive as a group. But David Lloyd George, brought to Parliament in a special election held because of the sudden death of an incumbent, stood alone. He was notably young, with a slight figure and a handsome, sensitive face. His youth was all the more apparent as he stood beneath the venerable figure of Lord Cottesloe, almost seventy years his senior. As he waited, he surveyed the august body of gentlemen and the hall that was to be the scene of his future labors.

Then, between two honorable members, he advanced to the Speaker's Table to be formally introduced. For a moment he was in the spotlight; all eyes were on him, and cheers and applause rose to greet him. Then he turned to find a seat on one of the back benches, where the rank-and-file members sat. It was the beginning of a great parliamentary career.

> *He loved the earth; he loved his native country ways; he was master of his native language. He was proud of all these qualities.*
> —EARL LLOYD GEORGE
> Lloyd George biographer

Members of the Gorsedd, or Assembly of Bards, participate in the 1894 *Eisteddfod*, a Welsh festival of arts and crafts that dates back to the 12th century. The festival was reestablished in the 19th century as part of the resurgence of Welsh national pride, which permeated the youth of David Lloyd George.

Lloyd George as a young boy of about five. He lost his father early and was brought up by his mother, Elizabeth, and uncle, Richard Lloyd, who encouraged the boy's precocious talents.

When Lloyd George entered Parliament, he was the representative of a relatively new phenomenon. The government of Britain had for centuries been in the hands of the privileged aristocracy. The 19th century had been notable for a series of bills on parliamentary reform enabling a much broader segment of the population to vote. The Reform Bill of 1867, for example, almost doubled the size of the electorate, adding 938,000 new names to the voting register, many of them workingmen in towns and cities. As a result, the political scene was changing. Lloyd George came from a background that set him apart from the majority of the members of the Commons. Although his background was by no means disadvantaged, his family was neither rich nor landed nor aristocratic.

Lloyd George's father, William George, came from Pembrokeshire in southwest Wales. While serving as headmaster of the local school in the little fishing port of Pwllheli, he met and married Elizabeth Lloyd, who came from the nearby village of Llanystumdwy and was working as a domestic servant in Pwllheli. To further William's career, the young couple had to move often. Their first child, Mary, was born in Lancashire, England. Soon after, they moved to the northwestern port city of Manchester, where William had been offered a temporary post in charge of a big school. It was there, on January 17, 1863, that David was born. In an attempt to restore his ailing health, William gave up teaching and returned with his family to a small farm in Pembrokeshire, where he contracted pneumonia and died after only a few months, just before the birth of their third child, William. David was less than 17 months old at the time.

William had been in poor health for some time, but his death was nonetheless unexpected. The young mother was left, far from relatives and friends, with a family and no adequate way of supporting them. Her brother, Richard Lloyd, came to their rescue. This remarkable man would take the place of a father for the children.

Elizabeth George was a stout Baptist, a member of the Disciples of Christ, a Nonconformist Protestant sect. She reared Lloyd George in an atmosphere of dissent from the established Church of England.

Richard Lloyd was a cobbler at Llanystumdwy, where he took his sister's family to live. There he enjoyed the status of a master craftsman. He employed others to work under him, and his business flourished. The family had some savings, and David's mother had a small income of her own. By the standards of Llanystumdwy the family was well-off.

Richard and Elizabeth belonged to a small religious community known as the Disciples of Christ, successors to the Scotch Baptists, an extreme Protestant sect. Throughout his adult life, he was the unpaid minister of the local chapter, where the children received their religious training. A deeply religious man, Richard was highly regarded for his wisdom and integrity. An avid reader, he loved discussion and presided over the village debating society. To some extent a frustrated politician himself, he was the first to recognize David's talents. He was also a sincere Welsh patriot and was openly radical in politics even before the secret ballot protected the predominantly middle- and lower-class Liberal voters from reprisals from Conservative landowners. (The rich landowning class in Wales saw the Liberals as a threat to their privilege. Tenants who voted Liberal were often evicted from their homes.) Under his tutelage, David grew up to cherish his national identity.

Richard Lloyd, a deeply religious, intelligent man, instilled in his favorite nephew a love of politics and a feel for the common man. In gratitude for his support, Lloyd George eventually added his uncle's surname to his own.

Wales was then in the throes of a nationalist revival. First invaded by the Romans, then repeatedly by the English, Wales nevertheless preserved its culture through the ages. Most notably, it preserved the Welsh language. While Ireland and Scotland have become predominantly English speaking (in spite of attempts to revive the Gaelic language), the Welsh language has survived and remains a badge of national identity and a source of pride to Welsh patriots. David Lloyd George liked to point out that in this land conquered by Rome, Welsh was still spoken as it had been in Roman times, while Latin was taught as a dead language.

Welsh culture, inextricably bound to the language, also had ties to religion. Elizabeth I, the 16th-century Tudor queen of Protestant England, decided to place Welsh Bibles and prayer books side by side with the English versions in all the churches of Wales. One effect was that Welsh became a language that was written and read as well as spoken.

Further development of the established church, or the Church of England, in Wales was not successful, however. Bishops for Wales were appointed in England, tended to be English, and spent as little time as possible in Wales. The church promoted the English language and sought to eliminate Welsh. The Welsh resented being drawn into the Anglican church by bishops unconcerned with Welsh culture and issues, and gradually the Welsh people turned to Nonconformism. Nonconformists, or dissenters, were those who refused to conform to the teachings of the Church of England. They instead became fervent Methodists and Baptists. This long tradition of dissent became a vital element of modern Welsh nationalism.

Another characteristic of the Nonconformist churches is a long tradition of social and political protest. This was fueled by the fact that the thoroughly anglicized Welsh landowning class overwhelmingly belonged to the Church of England. The Nonconformist belief in the equality of the human soul also led to a desire for other forms of equality. Nationalists looked to the revival of ancient Welsh tradition and beliefs, such as the idealized concept

How can I convey to the reader, who does not know him, any just impression of this extraordinary figure of our time, this syren, this goat-footed bard, this half-human visitor to our age from the hag-ridden magic and enchanted woods of Celtic antiquity.
—J. M. KEYNES
British economist

Lloyd George's admiration for Abraham Lincoln originated with his uncle, who kept a portrait of the U.S. president in his home. They both admired Lincoln's devotion to freedom and equality.

of the *Gwerin* — a community of equals dedicated to God, Beauty, and Truth. It was a myth that helped sustain the nationalist movement. Similarly, national festivals of music, culture, and poetry, known as *Eisteddfods*, were revived. The first national Eisteddfod was held in 1858.

All of these factors in the national revival were strongly in evidence in Lloyd George's day, and they influenced his development. His uncle, a Baptist committed to religious issues in Wales, was equally involved in their political ramifications and was always available and eager to discuss issues with his nephew. He was also an unfailing source of approval and encouragement. Because of this close bond, Richard Lloyd's last name became part of David's unusual surname, Lloyd George.

From his uncle, Lloyd George also gained a lifelong appreciation for U.S. president Abraham Lincoln. When Lincoln was assassinated in 1865, Richard Lloyd bought a portrait to hang in a place of honor in their home. The example of Lincoln and his opposition to slavery was also a major factor in arousing the strong Nonconformist opposition to English domination.

David and his brother, William, were both sent to the local village school, which was run, as were most Welsh schools, by the Church of England. Under the guidance and encouragement of the school's exceptional headmaster and teacher, David Evans, Lloyd George received an excellent education. Later, he was to say of Evans that "no pupil ever had a finer teacher."

His admiration for Evans, however, did not prevent young David from acting on his own convictions. In one example, a ceremony was held at the school of Llanystumdwy in which the children were examined in the Apostle's Creed and other Church of England teachings. Because this annual event was a popular public occasion, attended by important local personages, the children, nearly all of whom came from Nonconformist homes, had to participate. The ceremony was particularly offensive to the George children because it required them to assert that they had received their names at baptism, although as Baptists they would not undergo the sacrament until they were older. (David was twelve when Richard Lloyd performed the rite.)

David Lloyd George inspired his schoolfellows to action. When the moment came to recite the Creed, no one said a word. Such a display of disobedience was disconcerting and embarrassing to David Evans. As the tension mounted, it was William who finally broke down and led the other children in the Creed. David resolutely refused to say a word and is supposed to have thrashed his brother soundly for his weakness. The incident shows David's early political understanding as well as his ability to overcome personal feelings for a cause. Moreover, it was successful. The Nonconformist children were never again required to say the Creed.

With his natural precocity and with David Evans for a teacher, young David Lloyd George completed the seventh, and highest, grade and received advanced tutoring at age 13. The time soon came to decide upon his future, and law seemed a respectable career. He chose the profession of solicitor, a lawyer who advises clients, represents them in lower courts, and prepares cases for barristers to try in higher courts. A friend of his uncle introduced him

David Evans was headmaster and instructor at Lloyd George's village school at Llanystumdwy. Despite their religious differences, Lloyd George later praised Evans for his excellent teaching abilities.

Welsh schoolchildren pose for a portrait, 1905. Even as a child, Lloyd George was offended by the Anglican (Church of England) teachings in school and once inspired a protest of silent disobedience among his fellow students at a public ceremony.

to a firm of solicitors, where he studied as an articled clerk, or apprentice, for more than four years. The £100 cost of his training was a considerable expense for the family, but they paid it gladly.

The firm where David was apprenticed to work was in Portmadoc, a town some distance from Llanystumdwy, and for the first year he had to live in a rented room. Then Richard Lloyd sold his business, and the whole family moved to the town of Criccieth to be closer to David, who once again lived with them, often making the 10-mile round-trip on foot. To help with expenses, the George family took in lodgers in their new home during the summer season.

Compared with Llanystumdwy, Criccieth is a town of some substance. Situated in a beautiful position on Cardigan Bay, it commands views across the bay as well as of the beautiful mountains of Snowdonia to the north. The old town is clustered around the ruins of a 13th-century castle conquered by the famed Welsh rebel, Owen Glendower. More important to the inhabitants, the railway line that reached the town in 1865 enabled it to become a holiday resort for the wealthy English from the Midlands as well as local vacationers.

For Lloyd George, a young man of lively temperament, it was exciting to have broader horizons. Because of the flow of visitors, Criccieth was a step into a larger and more cosmopolitan world. Portmadoc was larger still. A flourishing port and trading and shipbuilding center, Portmadoc attracted people who had traveled to places Lloyd George had only read about.

The new law clerk had an office in the main street of Portmadoc. Much of the law he had to learn was of a humdrum order — such as the legal details of mortgages and fire insurance — useful nevertheless in the lives of ordinary men and women. When he passed his final Law Society examinations and was formally admitted to the Roll of Solicitors in 1884, he took the bold step of setting up an office of his own. At first his office was in the family home in Criccieth, but he soon found enough work to open an office in Portmadoc. William followed in his footsteps and joined him there two years later in the firm of Lloyd George and George. During these early years, David established a good reputation as a counselor advising barristers and as a fearless advocate representing tenant farmers and Nonconformists against the landowners and the Church of England.

Criccieth was also where he met his wife. Margaret Owen was the only child of Richard Owen, a substantial tenant farmer and one of Criccieth's most respected citizens, who traced his descent from Prince Owen Gwynedd, ruler of North Wales in the 12th century. His wife was from a prosperous farming family. Margaret's parents determined that she should have advantages that they themselves had not received. She went to a genteel girls' school, where she received a proper Victorian education, learning only what was considered suitable for a girl of the period. She was an amateur artist and a passionate gardener. The indulged daughter of devoted parents, she exuded self-confidence and was known for her easy manner and the way she was able to put people around her at their ease. Margaret was intensely proud of her background and loved Criccieth with a passion. Willful, used to having her own

As a young man Lloyd George studied law with a firm in Portmadoc, a town in northwest Wales. After apprenticing for four years and passing his examination, he opened his own firm.

As a child, William George was overshadowed by his talented older brother. He also pursued a legal education and joined Lloyd George's law firm, which he ran when his brother's political career took him to London.

way in everything, she was a spirited match for David Lloyd George.

The circumstances of their meeting are unclear, but they must have seen each other in and around Criccieth. David's diary reveals that he escorted her home from a debating-society function in 1884. He wrote her many letters over the next four years, progressing in tone from "My dear Miss Owen" to "My dearest little Maggie." They were both strong personalities, and their courtship had its difficulties, one of which was David's tendency for flirting with other women. He was always very attractive to women, and this was disturbing to Margaret. While in some way it added to his charms, she also feared that jealousy might make her unhappy. Her parents' reservations, apart from the fact that no one could be good enough for their daughter, were mainly religious. The Georges and Richard Lloyd were Baptists, and the Owens were Methodists. In addition, Lloyd George was skeptical of organized religion.

Despite her family's objections, Margaret ultimately decided that she could not give him up. The marriage took place on January 24, 1888, in a Methodist chapel outside of Criccieth. Richard Lloyd and the Methodist minister officiated jointly. Because of the religious difference, the Owens avoided the publicity of a Criccieth wedding and kept the occasion a private one. Nevertheless, the town was not to be deprived of its celebration. After Mr. and Mrs. Lloyd George had departed on their honeymoon, the town marked the occasion with a bonfire and fireworks.

Even while working as a solicitor, Lloyd George never thought of the law as his real interest. While still an articled clerk, he wrote frequently on politics for a local newspaper, the *North Wales Express*. He brought to the courtroom his already considerable experience as a debater in the Criccieth and Portmadoc debating societies. It was soon clear where his true bent lay, and he realized that it was possible to combine his legal and political interests.

Politics had long been the exclusive province of gentlemen, and for many it was an absorbing occupation. "When I am ill," wrote Sir William Harcourt, "I am in bed. When I am not, I am in the

House of Commons." Since the Reform Act of 1867, however, the arena had widened, not only allowing more people to vote but also making it possible for men such as Lloyd George to run for Parliament.

The Nonconformists had long given their allegiance to the Liberal party. Wales was strongly Liberal for nationalist reasons, as well; under British Prime Minister William Gladstone, the Liberal party promised more attention to the "Celtic fringe" — as Ireland, Scotland, and Wales were known because their traditional languages were Celtic. (At the time, all three were formally united with Great Britain.) The George family had always supported the Liberal party, so Lloyd George was a Liberal from his earliest years, by inheritance as much as conviction.

Fortune brought Lloyd George early fame. Just after his marriage in 1888 he handled a case that placed him in the public eye. It concerned the right of a Nonconformist family to be buried in a lot adjoining an Anglican cemetery in Llanfrothen. A bigoted Anglican parson denied the family right of burial and, after they defied him on the advice of Lloyd George, brought a case against them for trespassing. It was a great cause to champion, for in nationalist Wales breaches of the law against the Anglican church were seen as political acts of defiance. Lloyd George, as attorney, was instrumental in winning the judgment for the family, and he earned a name as a defender of the Welsh underdog. The case received much attention from the press, and overnight his name became known throughout Wales. With a reputation as a stirring public speaker, a vehement and rousing advocate for Welsh causes who was also good-humored and witty, his popularity quickly grew.

Lloyd George had been proposed as a candidate for Parliament for the first time in 1886, but he chose to wait before standing for election. At the time members of Parliament were not paid, and he felt he had to establish himself more firmly, both financially and professionally, before he could consider becoming a candidate.

He did not have to wait long, however, for a replacement was needed for the Liberal candidate

Margaret Owen was the strong, independent daughter of a prosperous tenant farmer in Criccieth, where Lloyd George lived while studying law. Despite the religious objections of her parents the two were married in January 1888.

An 1859 cartoon depicts British statesman Benjamin Disraeli, burdened by his Reform Bill, tripping over the bill's chief opponent, Prime Minister Lord Palmerston. In 1867 the Reform Bill passed, however, and extended voting rights and eligibility for elective office.

from Caernarvon Boroughs, who had lost the last election in 1885. The publicity from the Llanfrothen case brought Lloyd George to the attention of the party, and on December 20, 1888, he was selected, despite his age and inexperience, over two other candidates as the new Liberal candidate for the Boroughs.

During the first three years of their marriage, Lloyd George and Margaret lived in the home of her parents. Then Richard Owen built two houses side by side outside Criccieth, facing the sea. One was the home of Margaret's parents; the other was rented to Margaret and David and was the birthplace of their five children. In 1889 Richard Lloyd George was born. He was followed by Mair in 1890, Olwen in 1892, Gwilym in 1894, and the youngest, Megan, in 1902. But David Lloyd George did not have his heart set on a life in Criccieth.

Lloyd George's Welsh nationalism and local reputation as champion of the working class won him a seat in Parliament in 1890. He would be the liberal representative from Caernarvon Boroughs for 54 years.

He was called to Parliament earlier than anyone could have expected. In March 1890 the Conservative incumbent for Caernarvon Boroughs died suddenly of heart failure. This meant that there would have to be a by-election, one called between regularly scheduled elections, to fill his place.

Lloyd George had had little more than a year to prepare. However, he was familiar with the Boroughs and was already well known. The Conservative candidate had the disadvantage of stepping in at the last moment, but he, too, was a local man and well liked. He could stand before his constituents as a reassuringly mature candidate, but the outcome of the election was by no means a foregone conclusion.

Lloyd George fought his campaign largely on Welsh nationalism. He also exploited the fact that his opponent was from the squirearchy, the wealthy landed class. He declaimed, "The Tories have not yet realised that the day of the cottage-bred man has at last dawned." When the results were counted (and recounted), Lloyd George had secured his seat in Parliament by the astonishingly narrow margin of 18 votes. The people of Caernarvon that day added a great name to the history of their country.

2

A Man of the People

The British parliamentary system differs in several ways from the American system. Each party has a leadership and a structure of organization that remain in place whether the party is in power or in opposition. Furthermore, a cabinet minister or a prime minister arrives at that position only after many years in the party ranks. The cabinet is chosen by the prime minister from among his own political party, but unlike the U.S. cabinet, the cabinet in England can overrule the prime minister. When Parliament is in session, opposing cabinets (the opposition is known as the shadow cabinet and is chosen by the party leader) face each other from the front benches on either side of the Speaker's Table.

When Lloyd George entered Parliament, the Liberal party was in opposition, meaning that the Conservative party held a majority of seats in Parliament and had formed a government. Moreover, the party was going through a difficult period due to a recent split in its ranks. The leader of the party, William Ewart Gladstone, was then 80 years old. As a statesman, Gladstone brought to politics a strong-minded

Nationalism has nothing to do with geography . . . it's a state of mind.
—DAVID LLOYD GEORGE

As a young member of Parliament, Lloyd George devoted his energy to two issues of concern to his constituency: disestablishment (the restriction of the power of the Anglican church in Wales) and reform of the liquor licensing laws.

When Lloyd George took his seat in Parliament in 1890 the Conservatives were in power. Lloyd George would spend most of his early parliamentary career in opposition to the government.

moral concern based on deep religious belief. He had enjoyed a long career in Parliament and had already once retired from politics. However, he was so emotionally engaged in his country's affairs that retirement had proved impossible for him. He returned to his second prime ministry from 1880 to 1885, at which time he was well into his seventies. His strong sense of commitment led to the split in the Liberal party. Once he became convinced that Ireland, a Catholic country, should be free from domination by Protestant England and that nothing less than Home Rule, or self-government, would satisfy the Irish people, he threw his full support behind this one measure. Not all of his party agreed with him; another faction, led by Joseph Chamberlain, was equally strongly in favor of union with Ireland. After Gladstone, Chamberlain was the leading member of the Liberal party and the person most likely to succeed him, so the split was of profound consequence to the party's future.

As a result of the split among the Liberals, Gladstone became dependent on the support of the Irish and Welsh parliamentary members, making the Liberal party the party of the Celtic fringe. Since Lloyd George's base of support was Welsh, it was important that he take every opportunity to promote Welsh interests. At the same time, there was no doubt that Gladstone's emphasis was on Ireland.

There was one overwhelming obstacle to securing Home Rule for Ireland. The House of Lords, the upper house of Parliament, at the time had the almost unlimited ability to modify or obstruct any bill that passed by the Commons and also had the final power of veto. (The House of Lords is made up of the members of the British peerage, or nobility, and certain officials of the Anglican church. Its members are not elected.) The Conservatives dominated the House of Lords and tended to obstruct legislation put forward by the Liberals. It was clear from the start that the Lords would not tolerate Home Rule for Ireland. If the Liberal party was to make radical policy changes, it would have to settle the constitutional issue of the limits of the Lords' power.

The other important concern in government was social reform. The Liberal party had for a long time tried to follow a policy of individual freedom from legal and economic interference and had been associated with the school of thought known as *laissez-faire*, which opposed government interference in economic affairs beyond the minimum necessary to maintain peace and property rights.

William Ewart Gladstone was the leader and conscience of the Liberal party in the late 1800s. Elected to his fourth term as prime minister in 1892, Gladstone made Irish Home Rule — self-government in Ireland — the primary Liberal issue.

Joseph Chamberlain and his Union Liberals favored the continued union of Ireland and Great Britain and led the opposition to Gladstone's impassioned fight for Home Rule. The issue eventually led to an irreparable split within the Liberal party.

In the late 19th century, however, it became apparent that the problems of an industrial society — overcrowding, poverty, disease, exploitation — would require state intervention. In summing up the general consensus, a member of Gladstone's cabinet said he was beginning to doubt "whether it is possible to grapple with this enormous mass of evil in our society by merely private, voluntary, and philanthropic effort." He believed that "the collective force of . . . the State" would have to be used "to remedy things against which our social conscience is at last beginning to revolt."

While Home Rule for Ireland and social reform formed the basis of Liberal policy, they were not the most important issues for Wales, and the Welsh members in Parliament suffered from one great disadvantage. While the Irish members of Parliament were united, the Welsh members remained divided by jealousy and rivalry between the north and south interests. The one cause that had some hope of uniting them was disestablishment, which meant the severing of the ties between the Church of England and the British state, which officially protected and maintained the church. Yet another important issue to all Nonconformists was a need to reform the licensing laws by increasing the tax on liquor licenses and so reducing the overall number of pubs. Drunkenness was a serious problem throughout the country, particularly disabling and degrading to the working classes.

After moving to London, Lloyd George's first public speeches focused on these two issues. In London he addressed the Liberation Society on the cause of disestablishment. In Manchester he advocated reduction of the number of pubs, seeing in them the causes of all evil. The liquor trade, he said, "reeks with human misery, vice and squalor, destitution, crime and death." On both occasions, he was received by wildly enthusiastic crowds.

In those days politicians had to make their voices carry well, for there were no microphones. Lloyd George did not hold his audience with booming oratory. He had a light tenor voice, colored by a gentle north Welsh accent. He seldom raised his voice for emphasis, but his effect on his audiences was nonetheless electrifying. He held them with his fierce delivery, studded with a quiet, often deadly, sarcasm. While he spoke he gestured in a manner much more Gallic than English. He made an audacious maiden, or first, speech in Parliament in which he attacked Joseph Chamberlain and another major parliamentary figure, Lord Randolph Churchill. The members of Parliament immediately realized that the new member was someone to watch. The press responded favorably, and Gladstone himself was reported to have been "exceedingly delighted."

Lloyd George was not just a good speaker; he was also an excellent and skillful parliamentarian. When legislation concerning church clergy was introduced, he obstructed it by proposing amendment after amendment. He sought in this way to demonstrate that disestablishment was desirable. Above all, he felt that the educational system, in which public money was used to fund schools run by Anglican clergy, should be secularized.

Welsh coal miners discuss an impending strike over pints of beer at a local pub. Lloyd George supported licensing as a measure to control the consumption of alcohol in Wales, where drunkenness was a major problem.

Lloyd George addresses a crowd at Sutton in Ashfield, England. His ability to move large audiences resulted not from a majestic style of delivery but rather, in Winston Churchill's words, from his "fiery mocking tongue."

The Conservative Parliament that Lloyd George had joined in 1890 was dissolved in 1892. The Liberal party faced the voters with a platform, known as the Newcastle Program, that included Home Rule for Ireland, disestablishment in Wales, local veto on liquor sales, and proposals on the working hours and payment of members of Parliament. For the country at large, Home Rule for Ireland was the main issue of the campaign. Only in Wales was disestablishment more important, and Gladstone seemed to give his support to the issue.

While Gladstonians, including Lloyd George, achieved an overwhelming majority in Wales, the party did not win a victory in the rest of Britain. Gladstone was therefore dependent on the Irish and Welsh minorities to sustain his majority in Parliament. After Lord Salisbury, the leader of the Conservative party, failed to win a vote of confidence in the newly elected Parliament, Gladstone was invited to form his fourth, and last, ministry in August 1892. One particularly notable choice in Gladstone's cabinet, Herbert Henry Asquith, would be a significant figure in Lloyd George's career. Like Lloyd George, Asquith — the new home secretary —

came from a Nonconformist background and had entered politics young, without financial or social background. He had graduated from Balliol College, Oxford, where he had distinguished himself. A lawyer, like Lloyd George, he had helped clear the name of Charles Stewart Parnell, the Irish leader of the Home Rule party, during a famous libel trial in 1889. His efforts on behalf of Parnell boosted his career. Asquith's promotion to the cabinet while still under 40 was unusual.

Early in his term, Gladstone made a visit to Wales for the opening of a public footpath leading to the summit of Mount Snowdon, the tallest peak in the British Isles. This occasion was important for Lloyd George, who made all the arrangements for welcoming the distinguished visitor and appeared at several public gatherings with Gladstone. On this occasion, Gladstone was as impressive as ever. William George, who was also there, writes that it was "everyone's main passion to see and hear the most heroic figure in Welsh eyes. . . ." Nevertheless, when he mentioned Welsh issues, Gladstone was noticeably vague.

Home Rule for Ireland remained the great issue of Gladstone's ministry. He tirelessly pursued this goal, although he must have known it was doomed to failure. There was never any doubt that the House of Lords would veto the bill, which took up nearly all the available time in the first session of Parlia-

Supporters of Irish Home Rule take part in a torchlight march to Dublin in 1888. Home Rule was the major issue presented to the public in the 1892 Liberal party platform, known as the Newcastle Program.

ment. In September 1893 the proposal was thrown out by the House of Lords after a scornfully brief debate.

All the other items of the Newcastle Program received short shrift. A "suspensory" bill — intended to stop the creation of any new vested interests in the Welsh church pending disestablishment — and a bill designed to allow local control of liquor consumption in Wales received only limited attention.

Lloyd George drafted several letters to Gladstone from the Welsh M.P.'s (members of Parliament) expressing their increasing frustration and demanding that he make Welsh disestablishment his highest priority after Irish Home Rule. His conciliatory but noncommittal response prompted the Welsh members to discuss independence from the Liberal party. Lloyd George convinced them to delay their rebellion and reconsider their support of the government if the disestablishment measure was not forwarded to the House of Lords by the end of the parliamentary session.

Gladstone's last ministry was fraught with frustrations. Legislation was obstructed by the Conservatives in both houses, and Gladstone was unable to reach agreement within his own cabinet. After a last speech vehemently denouncing the House of Lords, Gladstone resigned on March 3, 1894, citing his age and failing health.

For 62 years in the House of Commons, the old statesman had been the embodiment of Victorian morality and conscientious public service. Through sheer force of character, he had raised political leadership to a high standard that would not be forgotten. All the same, Gladstone's legacy was a mixed one. He left the Liberal party in power but split over the Home Rule issue. A new joint leadership was formed by Archibald Primrose (Lord Rosebery) and Sir William Harcourt, but they could not easily solve the problem of Home Rule. The Liberal party needed the support of the Irish; it would be impossible to shelve the issue with honor, nor did a tacit agreement to abandon Home Rule make it possible to reunite the party with the Union Liberals, led by Chamberlain.

Herbert Henry Asquith was home secretary in Gladstone's 1892 Liberal cabinet. Asquith, who shared with Lloyd George a nonaristocratic background, would play an important part in shaping the young politician's career.

The Liberal party remained hampered by a small majority, an antagonistic House of Lords, and the loss of a great leader. Lloyd George remained skeptical about the party's renewed assurances to the Welsh members on the Welsh disestablishment bill. He thought the time had come for independent action. He called a meeting of his constituents and described the Liberal party's record on Welsh issues. He asked for their support to develop a new strategy, apart from party policy. He now took the stance of a Welsh nationalist in Parliament, and his policy became one of obstruction of the government until it fell. Rosebery's government, already weak, collapsed, and he resigned in 1895. In the general election that followed, the Conservatives, headed by Lord Salisbury, won a strong victory.

Within a very short time, Lloyd George had emerged as an independent thinker. He had put the interests of his country before those of his party and had proven an able defender of the rights of the Welsh. His rebellious action was not a handicap when he faced his constituents in the 1895 election. For the next ten years, with the Conservative party in power, Lloyd George's role would be as a backbencher in the opposition.

3

Her Majesty's Loyal Opposition

When Lloyd George was reproached for having made life so difficult for the Liberal ministry, he replied that if he had been sometimes "rather troublesome to a Liberal ministry in the cause of Wales," he would be "a hundred times more so to a Tory [Conservative] government."

With the Conservatives in power, he kept his word. As soon as Parliament was back in session, he took up the cudgel again, establishing his reputation in the House as a well-informed and forceful debater. He never took part in a debate without having acquired a thorough knowledge of the issues involved.

For some time he had been interested in a Welsh nationalist league known as *Cymru Fydd* ("Wales of the future" or "Young Wales"). Welsh politics were torn by disagreement and rivalries. Lloyd George hoped to bring unity by means of the league and to create a strong lobby for Wales, similar to the one that served the Irish so well. Though this never proved possible, addressing the league on Welsh is-

[T]he fact remains clear and undeniable that Mr. Lloyd George is the best fighting general in the Liberal Army.
—WINSTON CHURCHILL
British prime minister

Lloyd George and Margaret pose with their daughters, Mair (center) and Megan, 1904. Lloyd George's political career put a heavy strain on his family life, as Margaret refused to join him in London, considering it an unhealthy place for young children.

Horatio Herbert Kitchener (later Lord Kitchener) won fame for his 1898 military campaign to capture the town of Fashoda in the Sudan. Lloyd George, opposed to antagonizing French interests in the same area, alone spoke out against Kitchener's aggressive act.

sues gave him plenty of opportunity to develop and expound his own ideas, one of which was "home rule all round." By this he did not mean an independent Wales, but a measure of autonomy that would give the citizens of Scotland, Wales, and Ireland more responsibility in governing their own affairs. Again and again he claimed that central government was becoming too unwieldy. He blamed this on a greater amount of state interference overall, not on any one party.

In his argument for more autonomy, he repeatedly pointed out the need to appoint Welsh representation in matters pertaining to Wales. Even the Liberal government, supposedly pro-Welsh, included only one Welsh member when it appointed a commission of three churchmen on the question of disestablishment. Why were there no Welsh-speaking agricultural inspectors? Why no labor representative for North Wales on the Board of Trade? Why no Welsh-speaking surveyors employed for the preparation of Welsh maps? These questions brought Lloyd George positive attention from the press.

Lloyd George was quick to capitalize on the government's political errors. When the Conservatives introduced an education bill designed to bring some uniformity to the school system, he vehemently objected to the effects it would have on the Welsh. The bill gave much-needed organization to the system but in such a way that church-affiliated schools would receive larger grants of public money. In Wales many Nonconformist children would have no choice but to attend Anglican schools, thereby receiving instruction in the Anglican faith and attending Anglican services.

Parliamentary inequities were another target, especially plural voting, which granted more than one vote to certain classes. Fearing it might be overwhelmed by democracy, the government in 1867 had granted a second, sometimes even a third, vote to all university graduates, to owners of government bonds or savings bank deposits of £50 or more, to members of learned professions, and generally to other members of the wealthy and educated classes. Lloyd George objected to this, saying that the system gave "one vote, or probably no vote at all, to the man who handles the plough, and ten to the man who handles the riding whip . . . one vote to the busy bee, and ten to the devouring locust. . . . It is not the soil of the country, but the soul, which we want represented in the House of Commons." His scorn for the House of Lords was unremitting. "No testimonials are required [for membership]," he said. "There are no credentials. They do not even need a medical certificate. They need not be sound, either in body or in mind. They only require a certificate of birth, just to prove that they are the first of the litter. You would not choose a spaniel on these principles."

Nor did he fail to hold the Conservative government to its appointed task. Old-age pensions had been promised at the 1895 election but seemed to have been forgotten. When the government brought in a bill to give relief to the Anglican clergy, Lloyd George was the first to point out that such a measure favored only one section of the community. When he followed up his protest with a reminder to the government of its interest in the pensions, the government's resolve was strengthened. In May 1899 a committee was appointed to study the question, and Lloyd George was invited to be a member. It was unfortunate that war intervened and delayed action on this legislation.

Another event of note was Lloyd George's determined and independent action during the Fashoda affair. In 1898 General Horatio Herbert Kitchener (later Lord Kitchener) and his Anglo-Egyptian army had advanced up the Nile in an effort to secure territory for Britain in the Sudan. When he heard that a French expeditionary force was holding Fashoda, a village in southern Sudan, Kitchener led his force there and claimed Fashoda for Britain. Both countries wanted to claim the Upper Nile territory, and a crisis developed.

On this matter the Conservative and the Liberal front benches were in agreement: If France took a territorial interest in the Nile Valley, it would be considered an unfriendly act. It seemed only Lloyd George had a different attitude: "If we defeat France, we shall be defeating the only power on the continent with a democratic constitution," he said. "Two great democratic powers at each other's throats, the only countries where you have perfect civil and religious liberty in Europe quarrelling with each other to make sport for the titled and throned Philistines of Europe." By opposing the prevailing tide of nationalism and holding to a principle that others ignored, Lloyd George showed his character. France eventually yielded in the dispute.

Lloyd George's years as a backbencher made heavy demands on his family life. He spent an occasional summer with the family but was quite often separated from them for weeks at a time. Margaret's presence in London was rare, partly because of pregnancy and nursing babies but also because she disliked London and thought that it was unhealthy for young children.

Because most of Lloyd George's time was taken up with work and politics, the time spent with his children was precious, and he exerted himself to make the most of it. His son Richard remembers "unforgettable evenings" when the family sat "spell-bound as my father unfolded the thrilling narratives that Dumas, Hugo, and Scott and other notables of a bygone age had written."

Lloyd George loved to travel in Europe and was often disappointed that Margaret did not accompany him, but in 1895 they went for a memorable holiday to Scotland together. On this occasion he learned to play golf. He had always loved to take long walks while growing up in Wales. Golf combined his preferred form of exercise with an added purpose. He remained an enthusiastic if not very good golfer for the rest of his life.

The frequent separations left Lloyd George free to pursue his romantic adventures. Unsuited to isolation and solitude, attractive to women, Lloyd George quickly developed a reputation as a womanizer. At a time when romantic indiscretions ruined the careers of more than one prominent politician — Parnell, for example — Lloyd George was fortunate to avoid the same fate. As the years went by, he and Margaret gradually became estranged over his amorous entanglements.

His finances were another source of worry. Because members of Parliament had traditionally been men of means, the question of salaries had been irrelevant. Parliamentary reformers had come to realize that the lack of salary excluded any but the wealthy from a political career, but in the progress of parliamentary reform precedence was given to other matters — such as enlarging the pool of eligible voters and trying to equalize voting districts.

Lloyd George, although not exactly "cottage bred," was one of the first Parliament members to face the problem of actually earning a living. With a growing family, it was a nagging concern. The firm of Lloyd George and George obviously gained prestige from his name, but it was still his brother, William, who did the great bulk of the work. Although Lloyd George handled the firm's business in London, there remained a clear imbalance in the work load. In the end the Lloyd George family was largely maintained by the brother who stayed at home.

Because of this constant strain Lloyd George was

There was something in Lloyd George, a love of intrigue, a lack of fixed principle, a curious inconsistency.
—ROBERT BLAKE
British author

The discovery of gold and diamonds in the Transvaal colony in South Africa renewed tension between the Boers (descendants of the original Dutch settlers) and the British, who sought to control all the South African colonies. Pictured are late 19th-century miners in South Africa.

tempted to earn money by speculation, that is, making high-risk investments with the aim of gaining an immediate profit. In 1892 he invested, and persuaded others to invest, in a highly speculative gold-mining venture in Patagonia, a region in southwestern South America. The original investors soon began to have doubts about this venture but encouraged others to invest in the scheme so as to cover their own losses. The venture proved Lloyd George an incompetent businessman and gained him a reputation for financial unscrupulousness that followed him throughout his career.

In 1899 the enthusiastic traveler had an opportunity to journey in a new direction — Canada. At the invitation of the Canadian government, he covered the full breadth of the country and carried back with him an idea of the vast spaces and expansive

spirit found on the other side of the Atlantic. While he was in Canada war broke out in another part of the British Empire.

The first colony of South Africa, the Cape of Good Hope, had originally been settled by the Dutch. The colony was seized by the British in 1795 and then formally ceded to Britain in 1814 following the Napoleonic Wars. In 1843 the British added another region, Natal, on the coast, along the Indian Ocean, to the Cape Colony. The descendants of the original Dutch settlers, the Boers, had long been restive under British rule, especially when the British abolished slavery in 1833. Hoping to escape British control, the Boers made a famous march, known as the Great Trek, to the north, where they established two new states — the Orange Free State and the Transvaal. While the Orange Free State was granted independence by Britain in 1854, it took a revolt by the Boers within the Transvaal to gain their independence in 1881.

The discovery of gold and diamonds in the Transvaal brought a community of foreigners — called *Uitlanders* by the Boers — in search of wealth. The foreigners quickly outnumbered the Boers, whose president, Paul Kruger, refused to grant the foreign community political rights, although their taxes provided nine-tenths of the state's revenues.

The Cape Colony's most notable citizen was Cecil John Rhodes. He had arrived in 1870, the year that diamonds were first discovered there, and he turned out to be a phenomenal businessman. He succeeded in making himself the director of a mining company that produced most of the world's diamonds. When gold was discovered in the Transvaal in 1886, his company expanded to encompass the gold fields. Another company formed by him developed and settled the state of Rhodesia. But making money was not the only thing that interested him. In 1890 he became prime minister, and virtual dictator, of Cape Colony. In league with British politicians, notably Chamberlain, he hoped to unite all South Africa under the British flag.

Rhodes was largely responsible for the Jameson Raid, an unsuccessful uprising of the Uitlanders led

Paul Kruger became president of the Transvaal following the Boers' successful 1880 rebellion against Britain. Alarmed by the influx of mainly English-speaking outsiders (*Uitlanders*) who flocked to the Transvaal following the discovery of gold there in 1886, Kruger denied the Uitlanders political rights, arousing further British hostility.

Cecil John Rhodes (third from right) became the dictatorial prime minister of the British Cape Colony in South Africa in 1890. Rhodes, a mining magnate, was the force behind the 1895 Jameson raid, a failed attempt to overthrow the Boer Transvaal government.

by his friend Dr. Leander Jameson against the Boers in 1896. The raid ended as a humiliating experience for the British. Whatever trust had existed in South Africa between the British and the Boers was lost. Rhodes was discredited and could not hold political office, but he maintained control of his company.

In 1897 Chamberlain, then colonial secretary, appointed a new high commissioner to South Africa. Once again, the British hoped to establish a union of the four states and began negotiations. The British asked for enfranchisement of the Uitlanders. The Boers seemed to agree but insisted on autonomy in their own internal affairs. On both sides, however, there was an unwillingness to compromise, and the talks soon broke down. In October 1899 war was declared between the British Empire and the Boer republics.

By the time Lloyd George returned to England from Canada, the war had already begun. He had not previously taken a great interest in the problem of South Africa, but he was generally opposed to the Conservative party's imperialist policy of expansion. (At the time Britain maintained a great empire of overseas colonies; imperialism is the rule of one nation over other nations or societies. Expansionists advocated the extension of the British Empire.) He spoke out against it both in the House of Commons and from public platforms throughout the country. In doing so, he opposed not only the government's policy but the feelings fervently declared by many of his countrymen.

Lloyd George had sound reasons for his opposition. In the first place, he felt that the war was unnecessary and wasteful. Just when financing for social reform programs at home was urgently needed, funds were diverted to armaments. He was also one of the few to predict that the war would not be quickly won and would cost the country heavily in men and munitions. His position was more than vindicated. In terms of the cost to Britain, the war was far longer and more extensive than the government and the country had foreseen.

War broke out between Britain and the Boer republics in 1899. After early British setbacks, Frederick Sleigh Roberts (later Lord Roberts), a hero of British campaigns in India and Afghanistan, was appointed commander in chief of the British forces.

Boer soldiers defend a rail line. The Boers proved themselves consummate guerrilla fighters, and their tactics caused great problems for the traditionally trained British forces. The British responded by herding suspected sympathizers, including women and children, into concentration camps.

After early reversals, in 1900 the British sent two eminent soldiers, Frederick Sleigh Roberts (later Lord Roberts) and Kitchener, to win the war. Lloyd George's antiwar stand became increasingly unpopular, even in Wales. Criccieth itself reflected the intensity of the prevailing jingoism (belligerent nationalism) when effigies of Lloyd George, his brother, and his uncle were publicly burned. When Lloyd George went out in public, he did so at great personal risk. On one occasion, when he spoke at Bangor in North Wales, he was struck over the head with a cane. When he spoke in Glasgow, the meeting became so violent that he had to escape through the

back of the hall to avoid the flying chairs.

While military successes were being achieved abroad and the Liberal party was divided over the war, the Conservative government decided to capitalize on its popularity and called for a general election.

When the British army captured the archives of the Orange Free State and discovered a few letters from British M.P.'s to the Boer leaders, the Conservatives saw a way to discredit their opponents. The Colonial Office only hinted at the contents of the letters and refused to identify the authors, immediately focusing suspicion of treasonable actions on antiwar protesters like Lloyd George. When Chamberlain did not hasten to clear their names, Lloyd George attacked the prime minister, Lord Salisbury, for what seemed like deliberate opportunism and counterattacked hints of treason by revealing that a large number of War Office contracts had gone to a firm run by Chamberlain's brother. In a hard-fought election, Lloyd George won a larger majority than ever before, although the Conservatives remained in power.

The Boer War continued. The two Boer republics were occupied and annexed, and Kruger fled to Europe. The Boers, under Jan Smuts and Louis Botha, turned to guerrilla warfare, relying on irregular tactics like harassment and sabotage, and sustained the war. The guerrilla groups were supported by sympathizers on scattered farms throughout the countryside. The British retaliated by burning the farms and herding men, women, and children into concentration camps. The bases of support for the guerrillas were thus removed, but the retaliatory raids did not cease, and the camps became a new focus for criticism of the war. Lloyd George opposed the methods used and drew attention to the dreadful mortality rates at the camps.

Peace finally came, but not until the summer of 1902. Although the Transvaal and the Orange Free State became part of British South Africa, the terms of the Treaty of Vereeniging were generous to the Boers, allowing them to return to their farms and keep their rifles. Also, their language, *Afrikaans*, was given official sanction, and amnesty was granted to all but the leading rebels.

It would be completely false to suppose that because Lloyd George opposed the Boer War he was opposed to Britain's empire of colonies or to warfare. He regarded war as a terrible calamity to be avoided at all costs, but he was not a pacifist and was known to commend the use of armed force in some situations. His vision of the empire included independent self-government by the peoples within it, although with ties to Great Britain still maintained. He felt that a measure of freedom could hold together what imposed force would break apart. "We

Lloyd George vehemently opposed the British occupation of the Boer lands and the harsh conditions of the concentration camps. His stand was highly unpopular, and some of his speeches ended in violence.

ought to give freedom everywhere — freedom in Canada, freedom in the Antipodes [Australia and New Zealand], in Africa, in Ireland, in Wales, and in India," he said. "We will never govern India as it ought to be governed until we have given it freedom."

For two and a half years the Conservatives in power had struggled with an issue that threatened to split the party. This was caused by two different opinions on fiscal policy. Since 1846 the prevailing economic theory in Britain had been what is known as free trade — that is, no tariffs or duties (tariffs or duties are essentially taxes) were imposed on either imported or exported goods. Since trade in the second half of the 19th century had generally flourished, such a policy received strong support. But in order to pay for the Boer War, the government had to raise revenue and proposed a small duty on imported corn. ("Corn" was the general term for most grains used for flour.)

Chamberlain had for some time proposed a change of economic policy. His proposals had two main components. The first was that tariffs should be imposed to regulate trade and make British goods more competitive with foreign goods. The other, called imperial preference, advocated that preference be given to trade with the British colonies. Chamberlain felt that tariff reform, combined with preference, would achieve three things. It would protect the British economy against the increasing threat of European competition, provide a way to raise money for further social reform, and

Sir Henry Campbell-Bannerman, Liberal party leader, became prime minister in 1905. His powerful cabinet included Herbert Asquith, Winston Churchill, and Lloyd George, whom he appointed president of the Board of Trade.

promote economic and political ties within the empire. In 1903 Chamberlain resigned from the cabinet in order to publicly campaign for tariff reform. While Chamberlain's ideas attracted a following, the immediate difficulty in presenting them to the public was that they would inevitably have the effect of raising food prices, as tariffs would raise the cost of imported grain. Arthur Balfour, who had succeeded Lord Salisbury as prime minister in July 1902, was leery of pursuing a policy that would lose him public support. The dispute split the Conservative party. One of the most important of the Conservatives, Winston Churchill, opposed the reintroduction of the nominal duty on corn and joined the free traders on the issue. An admirer of Lloyd George, he was to become his staunch friend and ally.

Balfour attempted to steer a middle course on the question of tariff reform. Nevertheless, with a divided cabinet, his government was weakened. The Conservatives lost the 1905 general election, but they hoped that the Liberals, also divided on economic issues, would be unable to govern, thus returning the Conservative government to office. Such hopes, however, were soon confounded.

The new leader of the Liberal party, Sir Henry Campbell-Bannerman, became prime minister. Previously regarded as a slightly ineffectual politician, once appointed prime minister he acted decisively in putting together one of the ablest cabinets in British history.

Lloyd George had been recognized as one of the leaders of the Liberal party since before the Boer War. He was a popular platform speaker, and he had not spared himself in the party cause. Unlike most of his colleagues, Lloyd George thought nothing of giving up his weekends to politics. It was therefore no surprise when Campbell-Bannerman named him one of the members of the first Liberal cabinet to hold office in 11 years. On December 8, 1905, the prime minister asked him to be president of the Board of Trade, and Lloyd George, at the age of 42, began his career in high office.

The cabinet that Lloyd George joined boasted many illustrious men, including Herbert Asquith as chancellor of the Exchequer, Sir Edward Grey as foreign secretary, and Richard Burdon Haldane as secretary of war. Herbert Gladstone, the son of former prime minister William Gladstone, was appointed home secretary. Winston Churchill was invited to join the government as undersecretary to Victor Alexander Bruce (Lord Elgin) at the Colonial Office. One of the most remarkable of Campbell-Bannerman's appointments was John Burns as president of the Local Government Board. Burns had been a leader of the London dock strike of 1889 and was the first manual laborer to enter a British cabinet.

Once Campbell-Bannerman had secured his cabinet, he asked the king to dissolve Parliament and call for new elections. Accordingly, Lloyd George's first action as a minister was to return to Wales to seek reelection. As always, his first concern was to address issues that concerned his constituents. At the close of an address given in Caernarvon, he assured them that "of the nineteen men who constitute the cabinet nineteen are in favour of disestablishment." In fact, disestablishment was an issue that would have to wait. The House of Lords would never let it pass. But Lloyd George was sincere in speaking for the people, and he won an overwhelming majority. Throughout the nation, the Liberals won a landslide victory.

4

The Challenge of Office

The Parliament of 1906 was unusual in its makeup. The large number of professional, middle-class members was unprecedented. This was a Commons that would be sympathetic to the idea that members of Parliament be paid. As a member of the cabinet, Lloyd George would for the first time receive a salary; £2,000 a year seemed like riches.

Lloyd George realized that the voters had given the Liberal party a clear mandate. The makeup of the new House of Commons seemed to portray "a quiet but certain revolution, as revolutions come in a constitutional country, without overthrowing order, without doing an injustice to anybody, but redressing those injustices from which people suffer." The party was ready to commit itself to reform.

For his part, Lloyd George proved himself a supremely able administrator. During the next two and a half years he continued to make public appearances and to speak out as the Liberal party's most eloquent radical. At the same time he showed patience and resourcefulness in running a large government agency. Hardworking and unstinting with his time and energy, he was also willing to

He was a constitutional rebel in that he aimed to overthrow the existing social order and replace it with a more egalitarian social structure, by constitutional means.
—W. R. P. GEORGE
Lloyd George biographer

Lloyd George and Churchill set out for Parliament on budget day, 1910. As chancellor of the Exchequer under Prime Minister Asquith, Lloyd George was responsible for major financial and social reforms. In his famous "People's Budget" of 1909 he declared war on poverty in Britain.

delegate work to his juniors. Among his assets was the ability to choose the men who could best serve him and, above all, to listen to what they had to say. He always preferred face-to-face discussion to reading a prepared report and was quick to grasp the essential points of a matter. As well as supervising men drawn from the civil service bureaucracy, Lloyd George also made sure he had some Welsh representation on his staff. Not only was this good public

When a bill to provide for the safety of merchant seamen came to the Board of Trade, Lloyd George took the unprecedented action of securing the opinions of those affected by it — shipowners and seamen — before presenting the bill to Parliament.

relations, it was a way of keeping in touch with Welsh opinion.

The first piece of legislation on his desk when he took over the Board of Trade — a bill to ensure the safety and welfare of British seamen in the merchant navy — was inherited from his predecessor. It was nevertheless a matter of deep concern to him. Although some safety measures had already been made law, there was still need for more regulation.

Lloyd George came up with an original and unorthodox procedure to collect information for the bill. He turned to the people who would be most affected by the proposed legislation and invited representative shipowners to meet him at the Board of Trade. When he told them about the proposed legislation and asked for their views, they were astonished but welcomed the chance to participate. A few weeks later Lloyd George summoned the same group and offered them the draft bill for their comments. Such a display of confidence produced many valuable suggestions. It also helped to overcome objections to the bill before it was even presented to the House of Commons. Through this kind of cooperation Lloyd George achieved what he most cared about — the greatest benefit for the men who worked on the ships.

In the same year he proposed the Census of Production Act, a bill designed to gather statistics on the output of domestic industries. Looking ahead, he saw this as a necessary and valuable step for future economic policy. Again, he eased passage of the bill by seeking advice and support from the people most involved and showed himself willing to listen to their point of view.

He then set out to provide the country with a system of commercial intelligence. He knew that German and American businessmen were provided with information about trade in different parts of the world. Britain, however, lacked a system for getting that same kind of information to British businesses. He designed a scheme for circulating information gathered by British missions abroad that soon proved invaluable to the business community. He went a step further toward trade with Britain's major colonies, sending trade representatives to Canada, Australia, South Africa, and New Zealand.

He had already demonstrated tact and resourcefulness in avoiding conflict. In 1907 his skill as a conciliator was called upon in a matter of national importance when a national rail strike seemed imminent. The directors of Britain's railways and the Amalgamated Society of Railway Servants had reached a deadlock, and Lloyd George had to step in. As he confronted a meeting of the 17 chairmen and 12 general managers of the railway companies, Lloyd George, according to an eyewitness, transformed his "frigid, indifferent, barely attentive" listeners into an audience that was "almost meek." They were willing then and there to accept Lloyd George's proposals, which led to a settlement by negotiation.

The strike was ultimately called off. The country had been spared a damaging conflict, and Lloyd George was publicly congratulated by the prime minister and subsequently by the king and queen at Windsor Castle. He was, without doubt, the man of the hour.

While at the Board of Trade, he was also responsible for another important piece of legislation, which arose out of the need to create a single authority to govern the port of London. Three separate dock companies were interested parties, and bringing them together was no easy matter. Nevertheless, through negotiation and careful and detailed preparation, Lloyd George established the Port of London Authority.

A labor leader holds the attention of a crowd of unemployed in Dublin. On a trip to Germany in 1908, Lloyd George was impressed by the German system of social welfare, including unemployment insurance, and he returned convinced that Britain needed a similar program.

While he was at the Board of Trade his family moved to a house near Wandsworth Common in London. It meant a great deal to him to have them close at hand after years of separation. In spite of Lloyd George's dedication to his work, he and Margaret even enjoyed an occasional holiday together. He took particular delight in the presence of his oldest daughter, Mair, who was seventeen. Intelligent and musical, she was undoubtedly her father's favorite.

When several months later Lloyd George received a message that Mair had come home from school feeling ill, there seemed to be no reason to be overly concerned. Five days later Mair died after an operation for appendicitis. It was the single greatest anguish of his life, one that he never overcame entirely.

The sad event brought William to London from Criccieth. The family and Lloyd George's colleagues at the Board of Trade all rallied to support him. When Christmas came around, it was decided that a change was necessary. A trip with a friend and

Weary miners in Bargoed, Wales, wait to ascend to the surface with their coal. Lloyd George was a consistent advocate for working-class interests. His budget of 1909 proposed new taxes, aimed primarily at the wealthier classes, with the resulting revenue to be used for social programs for the poor and working classes.

his two sons and the two Lloyd George boys, Dick and Gwilym, helped distract him. At a time when an automobile was still something of a novelty, they motored together through France and spent Christmas Day in Nice. Lloyd George's natural resilience and good spirits helped to heal the wound, but the tragedy would never be forgotten. Whenever Mair's name was mentioned, tears would come to his eyes.

While her husband was abroad, Margaret arranged to move the family from Wandsworth to Cheyne Place in London. As it happened, their stay there was very brief, for within a few months, Lloyd George was summoned to occupy a well-known official residence.

In 1908 Sir Henry Campbell-Bannerman resigned, and Asquith succeeded him as prime minister. He in turn appointed Lloyd George to the post he had vacated at the Exchequer, or treasury department. The promotion meant that Lloyd George would receive an increase of salary from £2,000 to £5,000. Also, the family would take up residence in the official home of the chancellor of the Exchequer, No. 11 Downing Street.

There the Lloyd Georges maintained an unpretentious, unaffected household. Visitors to the chancellor's home remarked on the lack of artifice they found there. At the same time they were impressed by Margaret's good sense, easy manner, and simple dignity. Although she enjoyed her husband's success, she still preferred Criccieth to London, so now that their income was larger, Lloyd George built a new house for her there, called Brynawelon ("the Hill of Breezes"). It had a marvelous site overlooking the bay, and Margaret, who was known for her green thumb, created a beautiful garden to surround it.

As head of the Exchequer, Lloyd George directed one of the most complex agencies of government. He came to his new post at a time of difficulty. The government's popularity was no longer at the peak it had attained in 1906, and an economic recession had set in during 1907. Many people were apprehensive of the changes they felt would occur now that the Liberal party had a chancellor of the Exchequer who was a confirmed radical.

> *I was elected as a liberal and to that creed I am pledged.*
> —DAVID LLOYD GEORGE

A 1910 cartoon satirizes the self-interest of the House of Lords. The Lords' veto of the People's Budget created a constitutional crisis when the Commons introduced a Parliament Bill to permanently limit the power of the upper house.

Lloyd George's first task as chancellor of the Exchequer was the institution of old-age pensions. In a policy defined over three budgets, Asquith had been cautious about committing money to the party's declared policy of relief for the poor, and the issue of pensions had therefore been postponed. This delay, however, cost the party support in the country. Liberal policy had to be radical enough to appeal to those who would otherwise turn to the new Labour party, formed in 1900 as a federation of working-class organizations and interests.

Lloyd George had been committed to the introduction of old-age pensions since 1895, when the whole question had been preempted by the Boer War. Now, as chancellor of the Exchequer, he pushed for pension legislation, finding the necessary money in a new tax. In 1908 the government passed the modest but popular Old Age Pensions Act, which provided pensions to people over seventy.

Lloyd George next tackled the enormous task of the 1909-10 budget. Not only was there a new program of wide-ranging social reform to be funded but the Board of Admiralty had submitted huge estimates. The growth of German naval power was causing alarm, and the Admiralty was anxious to maintain British supremacy at sea. The opposition could be counted on to throw its support behind the Admiralty. For these reasons, the budget was larger than it had ever been before, with an anticipated deficit of £16 million.

The opposition had for some time promoted a policy of tariff reform as a way of strengthening the economy and paying for social programs. The Liberal party had always resisted any deviation from a long-standing policy of free trade — that is, no tariffs or duties on imports or exports. Therefore, it was not possible for Lloyd George to use this method of raising money.

He proposed instead a program of taxation that was radically innovative, since it made heavier demands on the rich. His budget included a "super-tax" on incomes of £5,000 or more. He instituted taxes on land, on unearned profit due to an increase in land value, and on land that had rich mineral assets. In these proposals, he was tapping the resources of the wealthy that had grown as a result of industry and development.

He also proposed taxation of luxuries. The new motorcars, which only the rich could afford, were to be taxed, as was gasoline. Taxes on liquor and tobacco were to be increased. Much of the revenue derived from all these taxes would be used for social programs to benefit the poor.

Even before his budget was presented to the House of Commons, he encountered opposition in the cabinet, but he had the strong support of Winston Churchill and, above all, of Prime Minister Asquith, who stood by his chancellor's proposals.

April 29, 1909, was budget day in Parliament. Lloyd George introduced his budget in a marathon four-and-a-half hour speech. Due to its length, his speech had to be carefully prepared and read aloud, a style of oratory with which Lloyd George was un-

The roots of his social concern were imbedded in the soil of his native Caernarfonshire, in the deprivations which his family and himself had suffered and were still enduring.
—W. R. P. GEORGE
Lloyd George biographer

accustomed and uncomfortable. As a result, the momentous "People's Budget" was presented quite unlike his usual entertaining speeches. But in his spirited conclusion, in which he proclaimed the need "to wage implacable warfare against poverty and squalidness," he said, "I cannot help hoping and believing that before this generation has passed away we shall have advanced a great step toward that good time when poverty, and the wretchedness and human degradation which always follow in its camp, will be as remote to the people of this country as the wolves which once infested its forests."

The bill nevertheless met opposition on both sides of the House. Lord Rosebery, a Liberal, said it represented a revolution, but he undoubtedly suffered the bias of the rich. The Conservative opposition continued to propose the alternative of tariff reform and accused the government of introducing socialism, a system that favors social service, government ownership, and an equitable sharing of resources over private ownership.

In response to this challenge Lloyd George felt it necessary to make a strong statement in defense of the government's fiscal policy. For this he needed a public platform. He went to address a large crowd of workingmen in the East End of London. There, at a place called Limehouse, to an overflow crowd, he made one of the most famous speeches of his long career.

He spoke of the workingman's contribution to the nation's economy and the need to protect that workingman from the catastrophes that could wipe out a lifetime's hard-earned savings. Provision must be made, he said, for sickness, unemployment, and old age.

Then he went on to illustrate the wealth that he was proposing to tap in the interests of the whole society. He pointed to enormous profits drawn from the mere ownership of land by people who had themselves done nothing to increase its value. The two most obvious cases were the landowners whose property had been developed by the commerce and industry of others and the landowner whose land contained rich minerals, such as coal. To these ex-

King George V assumed the throne in 1910. His threat to swell the ranks of the Lords with new Liberal peers, or nobles, assured the passage of the bill that eliminated the Lords' unlimited veto power.

amples he contrasted the people whose industry and enterprise created the wealth, and the miners who faced every peril in order to fetch the coal to the surface. "We are placing burdens on the broadest shoulders," he said. "Why should I put burdens on the people? I am one of the children of the people. I was brought up amongst them. I know their trials, and God forbid that I should add one grain of trouble to the anxieties which they bear with such patience and fortitude."

The speech caused great offense in high quarters. Aristocrats accused Lloyd George of inflaming the masses to achieve his own ends. He was told that King Edward VII was not at all happy and had to write to the king justifying, but not apologizing for, the tone of his speech. Conservative opposition was strong, and the threat remained that the House of Lords would veto the finance bill. Asquith and the king had considered this possibility, and the king had promised the prime minister his support in making every effort to secure passage of the bill through the House of Lords. For centuries tradition had held that the Lords could not amend a money bill. However, there was no question that the "People's Budget" was a threat to the upper house.

Kept company by his pet pug, Lloyd George reads his correspondence. His home life was complicated by his frequent womanizing, which estranged his wife, Margaret. While at the Exchequer he employed Frances Stevenson as his secretary. She became his mistress and later his wife.

The aristocrats saw it as an attack on their purses, and many peers who had never bothered to attend the House of Lords before made this a special occasion to cast their votes. As the prospect of the Lords' veto appeared more likely, Lloyd George rallied again to the attack. In an October 9 speech at Newcastle, he said, "Let them realize what they are doing. They are forcing a revolution, and they will get it."

The budget was passed by the House of Commons on November 4. The Lords delayed some weeks before opening its debate, which took five days. Finally, it passed a motion stating "that this House is not justified in giving its consent to this bill until it has been submitted to the judgment of the country."

The rejection by the Lords created a constitutional crisis. Prime Minister Asquith introduced a resolution in the House of Commons asserting that the action of the peers was "a breach of the Constitution and a usurpation of the rights of the Commons." He asked the king to dissolve Parliament, and a general election was called for 1910.

The results, which did not bring a clear victory for either party, returned 275 Liberals, 273 Conservatives, 82 Irish Nationalists, and 40 Labour members to Parliament. It is true that on the question of limiting the power of the House of Lords the Liberals would have the support of the Irish and Labour members. Nevertheless, the Liberals had not gained a decisive victory.

The Commons passed a Parliament Bill to permanently limit the powers of the House of Lords, giving the upper house the power only to delay bills passed by the House of Commons. Money bills could only be delayed for one month; all other bills could be delayed for two years. The bill also proposed a mandatory general election every five years rather than seven. The whole question now hinged on whether the House of Lords would vote for limiting its own power.

The year ended with no action taken on either the budget or the Parliament Bill, and the government prepared for a renewed effort for 1910. However, in May, King Edward VII died unexpectedly. The new king, George V, made a plea to all parties for a compromise on the constitutional issue. A number of Liberal and Conservative leaders were agreeable to such a compromise, afraid that the new legislation would result in too radical a change of the constitution. None of Lloyd George's colleagues in the cabinet wanted to see a single-chamber Parliament. A series of confidential conferences resulted, but no agreement was reached.

The government's immediate concern now became passing the budget. Fortunately for Lloyd George, this time it was accepted by the House of Lords, which had come under increased pressure as a result of its previous veto. Predictably, however, the House of Lords then threw out the Parliament Bill, and Asquith asked the king to dissolve Parliament and call another election — the second in one year.

The specific issue presented to the electorate was whether the power of the House of Lords should be curbed. If the Liberals were returned to power, the king had secretly agreed, as a last resort, to create as many Liberal peers, or nobles, as would be needed to pass the Parliament Bill through the upper house.

In addition, there were two other important commitments the Liberal party made before going to the polls. The first was to Home Rule for Ireland, and the second was to the Women's Suffrage Bill, which would extend the vote to women.

For the twenty years of Conservative rule [the House of Lords] had caused no trouble at all; now that the Liberals had an overwhelming majority in the lower house, the peers became the chosen and willing instrument of the Conservative leaders who were powerless in the Commons.
—R. K. WEBB
American historian

Suffragette leader Christabel Pankhurst in her London office. Asquith and the Liberal party verbally committed themselves in 1910 to giving women the right to vote but delayed introducing the necessary legislation.

The results of the December election were almost the same as in the previous one — a disappointment to both major parties. When the new Parliament met in February, the Parliament Bill was reintroduced. This time the House of Lords simply destroyed it with amendments. Emotion ran high when the bill came back to the Commons. When Asquith rose to move rejection of the amendments, the opposition benches greeted him with jeers and catcalls. For half an hour, he was unable to speak. It was the first time in British history that the prime minister was so treated.

Asquith next spoke privately to Conservative leaders about the king's promise to create more peers. The leader of the Conservative party, Balfour, brought his powers of persuasion to bear on the upper house. Rather than be flooded with a large number of peers appointed by the king on the advice of the Liberal party, the Lords finally gave in and passed the bill by a vote of 131 to 114. The preeminence of the House of Commons was established. Another measure voted into law the same day had great significance for the House of Commons. A decision had been made to pay all members £400 a year.

After the conflict, the Conservative party decided upon a change of leadership. Balfour was forced to resign, and Andrew Bonar Law succeeded him. Bonar Law had been born in Canada. His father was a Presbyterian minister from Ulster, the northernmost of Ireland's provinces, and his mother came from Scotland. When he was 12 he moved to Scotland for his education. He had come to politics via a successful business career. He and Lloyd George, while members of opposing parties and of very different temperaments, had much in common. Neither belonged to the traditional ruling class. They also had a sympathetic understanding for each other that would lead in the future to an eminently successful partnership.

In the new government, Lloyd George remained at the Exchequer, and Churchill became home secretary. Together they were responsible for a groundbreaking bill to provide national health and unemployment insurance.

In 1908 Lloyd George had visited Germany and studied the system of social welfare that Chancellor Otto von Bismarck had established during the 19th century. Impressed by what he had seen, he returned to England convinced that a contributory system for calamities that could afflict the poor was urgently needed. The national health insurance plan he now proposed was a contributory one. Each employee would contribute fourpence a week, each employer threepence, and the government twopence. Insurance was to be made compulsory for all workers over the age of 16 who earned below £160 a year — about 15 million people. They would be provided with medical treatment, sick pay, and a disability benefit that could continue indefinitely. The measure was approved by Parliament in 1911.

During this time, Lloyd George also persuaded King George to revive the traditional ceremony installing the king's oldest son as the Prince of Wales, and he proceeded to tutor young Prince Edward, the future Edward VIII, in Welsh. At Caernarvon Castle on July 11, the investiture of Prince Edward as the Prince of Wales took place. The young prince was the first holder of the title since its institution in 1301 to address the vast crowd in Welsh.

I hope our competition with Germany will not be in armaments alone . . . to put ourselves on a level with Germany is to make some further provision for the sick, for the invalid, for widows and orphans.
—DAVID LLOYD GEORGE

Another event of this year was to touch Lloyd George closely. His youngest daughter, Megan, had received a rather fragmented education. Her parents decided to send her to a boarding school, but she would need some tutoring in order to take the examinations. Mair's former headmistress recommended a young teacher who had also been a schoolmate of Mair's. Frances Stevenson was a graduate of the University of London and was an extremely efficient secretary. She was interviewed by Lloyd George in London and immediately left for Criccieth.

Frances formed a very important relationship with Lloyd George that lasted the rest of his life. She became his private secretary and his mistress, and after Margaret's death, near the end of his life, she became his wife. Her keen interest in politics and history led her to preserve and catalog a vast archive of Lloyd George's papers, which have proven to be a valuable treasure for historians.

A notable characteristic of the period immediately before World War I was the growing militancy and violence among political groups. Much of the Liberal cabinet's time was spent in an effort to preserve law and order and prevent strikes. Union leaders challenged the government, as did the suffragettes (supporters of voting rights for women) and the Ulstermen, the Protestant minority in Northern Ireland (Ulster) who opposed Home Rule.

The suffragettes had been militant for some time. In 1905 they began a program of interrupting Liberal speakers with the cry "Votes for Women." The heckling was limited to Liberals because the leaders of the movement felt that only the Liberals would be likely to give women the vote.

Lloyd George was himself in favor of giving the vote to women. However, the issue presented a great difficulty to the Liberal party. If women were given the vote on the same selective basis as men, votes would go to women who were property owners, and the Liberals feared this would increase the Conservative vote. The only solution would be to give the vote to all adults, but there was little popular pressure for this. As a result, the Liberals gave priority to other reforms.

After 1910, when no action had been taken on behalf of their cause, the suffragettes became more violent. They began a deliberate policy of window-smashing. When they were arrested they insisted on going to jail, and there they went on hunger strikes. When the government instituted a policy of forced feeding, it was denounced for its brutality and the women were released. They then resumed the window-breaking campaign.

The two leaders of the movement at the time were Emmeline Pankhurst and her daughter, Christabel. Christabel directed policy from her hideout in Paris. "The argument of broken glass," as Emmeline Pankhurst called it, soon gave way to more violent methods. Empty houses were burned, including one that had been given to Lloyd George near London. As it was suffragette policy to burn only empty buildings, no one was hurt in the fire; Lloyd George had been away at the time.

Many workingmen also resorted to violence out of frustration. In spite of a healthy economy, wages had not kept up with rising prices. Peaceful methods did not seem to be effective, and mass labor strikes in 1911 and 1912 grew violent. Troops were called in on several occasions, which led to even greater rancor and violence and resulted in loss of life.

The Women's Municipal party meets to promote a local borough candidate. When the Liberal party continued to ignore their demands for the vote, the suffragettes turned to window smashing and property burning.

Ulster Unionists march to protest Asquith's new Home Rule Bill in 1912. Religious and political divisions between the Protestant north and Catholic south prevented any agreement on Home Rule, and by 1913 both sides were arming their citizens and raising militias.

In the midst of the turmoil, Lloyd George faced a crisis of his own — the so-called Marconi Scandal. Lloyd George and other Liberal leaders were accused of corruption in their dealings with the Marconi Wireless Telegraph Company, a London firm that received a lucrative government contract in 1912 to establish radio communications with all parts of the empire. Critics charged that the bidding was unfair and that Lloyd George and other Liberals subsequently profited from stock deals involving Marconi's American subsidiary. The crisis almost forced Lloyd George's resignation and the collapse of the government. In the end, the Liberal-dominated Parliament cleared Lloyd George of any deliberate wrongdoing, but his reputation had been severely damaged.

During the year he was under fire, he received loyal public support from Churchill, who vehemently defended him. Nevertheless, this partnership, too, was under strain. The two friends were in conflict because of the estimates Churchill, now first lord of the Admiralty, had submitted for the navy. Churchill emphasized (rightly as it turned out) the need for preparedness and the overwhelming importance of a strong navy for Britain — especially in view of the threat of an increasingly belligerent Germany. Lloyd George, however, did not fear war in Europe and considered the money better spent on social reform. Churchill rejected all compromise and threatened resignation. In the end the cabinet supported Churchill's position, but the active peace movement in England lent popular support to Lloyd George's position.

The Liberal party was still committed to Home Rule for Ireland, and the time had come to meet its obligation. This difficult, complex question came to the forefront again in April 1912, when Asquith introduced a new Home Rule Bill. It was not radical enough to satisfy the extreme Irish nationalist and republican movement, yet it went too far for the Protestant Irish in Ulster. The Ulstermen wanted a clear separation from the south of Ireland, which was overwhelmingly Roman Catholic. In September 1912 the rebels of Belfast signed a declaration to defeat Home Rule. Both sides in Ireland were beginning to raise and drill volunteers. It gradually became clear that if Home Rule became law, it would have to be defended by force. The British army in Ireland made it clear that the officers would not be willing, in such an event, to march against Ulster. The House of Commons was violently divided on the issue, and angry members frequently disrupted debate. In 1913 an amendment to the Home Rule Bill was proposed to exclude Ulster, but it was rejected, and both sides in Ireland continued to arm themselves.

Germany was supplying arms to both sides in Ireland, and clashes between opposing factions led to more violence. Civil war loomed. In July 1914 the king called all the party leaders to Buckingham Palace. Lloyd George and Asquith served as the government's representatives. While the conference leaders sought a compromise solution in London, the violence continued. In just a matter of weeks, however, Britain would be drawn into a far greater conflict that would claim the energies of Lloyd George for the next four years.

5

In Time of War

The assassination of Archduke Ferdinand of Austria on June 28, 1914, by a Serbian nationalist triggered an explosion that had been building since the late 19th century among European powers. A rampant spirit of nationalism, as well as intense economic and territorial competition, had created tension and mistrust among Germany, France, Great Britain, Russia, and Austria-Hungary. Austria-Hungary used the assassination as an opportunity to suppress Slav nationalism and declared war on Serbia on July 28.

Entangled by alliances, Germany, Russia, Great Britain, and France were soon drawn into the spreading conflict that became World War I, or the "Great War." Britain's decision to enter the war was based on two concerns that have preoccupied it through history: to protect the neutrality of the Low Countries — a strategically important area of northwest Europe, including the Netherlands, Belgium, and Luxembourg — and to prevent the ascension of one dominant power on the European continent.

He alone displayed courage when everybody else was knocking at the knees.
—WINSTON CHURCHILL
on Lloyd George's
wartime leadership

This famous World War I recruiting poster features the stern face of Secretary of War Kitchener. Kitchener's disastrous mishandling of Britain's war policy would help propel Lloyd George into the highest office in the country.

Bound by treaties, Great Britain, France, and Russia were known as the Allies, while Germany and Austria-Hungary were called the Central Powers. Although tied to Germany and Austria-Hungary by terms of the Triple Alliance agreement, Italy refused to fight with the Central Powers and joined with the Allies in 1915. The United States entered the war on the Allied side in 1917, while the Ottoman Empire (Turkey) fought with the Central Powers. Many smaller European countries also participated, most with the Allies.

When Germany invaded Belgium on the morning of Tuesday, August 4, the British government mobilized its army and sent an ultimatum to Germany demanding the withdrawal of all German troops from Belgium by midnight. As the time limit ran out, Sir Edward Grey, standing by a window in Whitehall and looking out into the night, spoke the words that marked the end of an era: "The lamps are going out all over Europe. We shall not see them lit again in our lifetime."

World War I began with the assassination of Archduke Franz Ferdinand of Austria in June 1914. Two months later, outraged by the German invasion of neutral Belgium, Great Britain entered the "Great War."

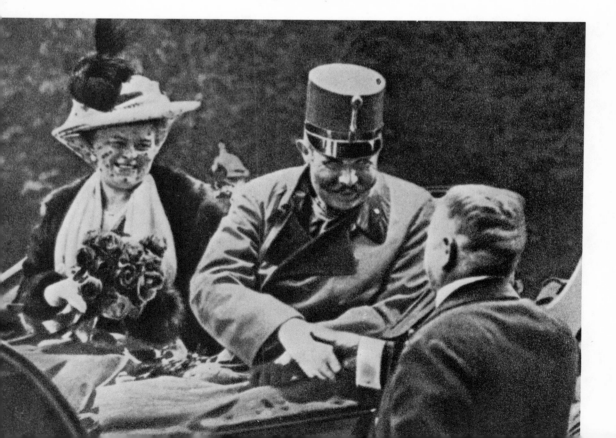

Lloyd George was a talented administrator in Britain's wartime government. He skillfully arrested the initial financial panic caused by the war's outbreak and took repeated action against bureaucratic mismanagement.

While the people of London, like the people of Berlin, Vienna, Paris, and St. Petersburg, looked toward the onset of war with patriotic fervor, the mounting excitement had immediate repercussions in the financial world. Big business fluctuated between panic and paralysis. During the days immediately preceding the declaration of war, the cabinet had been sitting in almost continuous session. Lloyd George struggled day and night to calm the financial panic caused by the threat of the war.

Lloyd George devised a delaying tactic to give him the time he needed. He declared the first few days of the war bank holidays and, with the help of expert advice from treasury officials and London's most prominent bankers, was able to take steps to steady the nerves of the financial world. These included an appeal to the public not to hoard gold and a reduction of the bank interest rates from 10 to 6 percent. The necessary bills were passed by both houses, and by Friday the banks opened to steady business. The panic was over.

Across the English Channel, the German army continued with its invasion. Its plan, developed by Field Marshal Alfred von Schlieffen, was to advance through Belgium and northern France and capture Paris in six weeks. The British Expeditionary Force — described by Kaiser Wilhelm II of Germany as "contemptibly small" — and the French army were unable to halt the advance until it reached the Marne River near Paris. There, the defensive line held. Facing that line, the German army created its own defenses, and a long campaign of trench warfare, marked by tremendous casualties, followed.

Although the war's fighting was centered in Europe, along the western front, in northern France and Belgium; and the eastern front, along the Russian borders; campaigns also took place in Italy, the Balkans, and the Middle East.

German soldiers advance through France. The German war strategy called for a quick offensive through Belgium and northern France to capture Paris within six weeks.

THE WESTERN FRONT 1914—1918

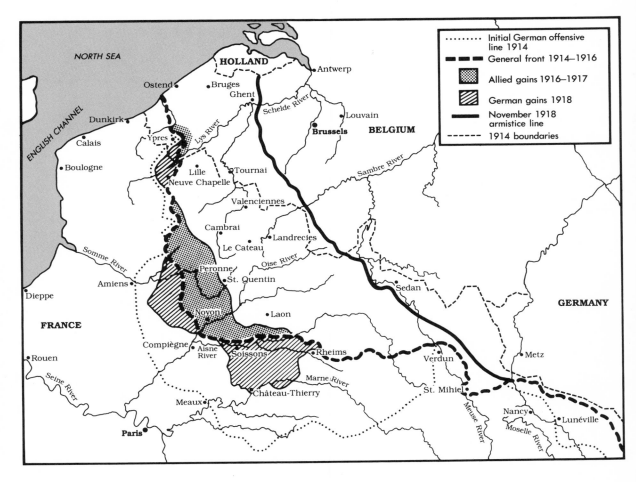

In Britain, Prime Minister Asquith asked Kitchener to become secretary of state for war. It was a fateful appointment. Kitchener was convinced that war was no matter for civilians to meddle in and did not feel compelled to let his colleagues in the government know everything that was happening in his department. When one of his field commanders sent desperate appeals from the front asking for ammunition, Kitchener maintained a perverse silence. Under the guise of "military secrecy," he failed to keep other cabinet members informed of the true state of the war.

The western front remained relatively stationary for much of the war. After the initial German thrust was checked at the Marne River, the war degenerated into a stalemate in the trenches, with little ground gained at the cost of many lives.

King George V (left front) tours Woolwich arsenal. To circumvent the uncooperative War Office, Lloyd George fought to establish a "shell committee" to investigate the serious shortage of munitions at the front.

The information that did reach the cabinet from other sources was unreliable but disturbing. It came from accounts given by soldiers coming home on leave or from war correspondents. The press at that time was not allowed near the front, so that source of information was no more reliable than any other.

Lloyd George, meanwhile, had to draw up a war budget. It was he, more than enyone else, who wanted information on the munitions that would be needed. He and Kitchener were in constant conflict. Lloyd George urged that a "shell committee" be appointed for the sole purpose of looking into the question of ammunition and supplies. Kitchener opposed him so violently that for a while the cabinet felt compelled to let the matter rest, but Lloyd George persisted in the charge that the ineptitude at the War Office was costing lives.

The disappointments and defeats of the first months of the war brought a change in the spirit of the country. Men and boys had marched cheerfully to fight for king and country, expecting to be home by Christmas. Instead, there had been a steady report of defeat and retreat, and the only result, after the long lists of dead and wounded, was a stalemate.

In 1915 Churchill urged a totally different approach on another front. It was a bold idea, but it led to disaster. Churchill's plan — to capture the Dardanelles, an important sea gateway, held by Turkey, connecting the Sea of Marmara and the Aegean Sea, and seize Constantinople — was flawed from the start by delay and indecision. Finally, after an Allied expeditionary force failed to dislodge Turkish troops defending the Dardanelles, the maneuver was abandoned. The British suffered more than 213,000 casualties there between April 1915 and January 1916.

Another scandal soon broke that reinforced the growing concern that the war was being mishandled. In March 1915 Field Marshal Sir John French sent a communication that confirmed Lloyd George's fears of mismanagement at the War Office. He was unable to continue his advance on Neuve-Chapelle in France — where nearly 13,000 British soldiers died to gain one square mile — for want of ammunition. He wired: "I desire to say with all the weight of my authority that the object of H.M. Government cannot be attained unless the supply of artillery ammunition can be increased." As Lloyd George had forcibly pointed out, "What we stint in material we squander in life."

Kitchener, however, continued to keep information from the prime minister and cabinet. Lloyd George persisted in his conviction that not enough was being done to mobilize the country to produce munitions and threatened to resign unless the prime minister took action. As a result, he was allowed to design a new Defense of the Realm Act. When enacted, it would empower the government to regulate industrial production and, if necessary, to take over any factory or workshop to aid the war effort. A shell committee was appointed on April 8.

The problems in the War Office and a new crisis in the navy department — the resignation of Lord Admiral John Fisher over Churchill's Dardanelles fiasco — led to a lack of confidence in the government's management of the war. The Conservative party leaders, Bonar Law and Lord Lansdowne, called for the prime minister to resign. Asquith was forced to form a coalition and admit the Conservatives. As part of the reorganization, Churchill lost his place in the government. Lloyd George was named head of a brand-new Ministry of Munitions.

Canadian troops man the trenches. Soldiers from the British Empire dominions, including Canada, Australia, and New Zealand, joined the British campaign. Their loyal service only increased Lloyd George's efforts to ensure that the armies were properly supplied.

A young German soldier poses in full uniform. The optimism of both sides that the war would end in a matter of weeks soon gave way to despair as the conflict dragged on through a second year and a staggering number of combatants were killed or wounded.

When Lloyd George arrived in his new offices, the furniture of the ministry consisted of two tables and a chair. That day he received an American visitor, Colonel Edward M. House, a close advisor of President Woodrow Wilson. They began with a friendly argument as to who should sit on the chair or on the table. Later, the colonel wrote to Wilson, "He spoke again and again of military red-tape which he declared he would cut as speedily as possible. He was full of energy and enthusiasm, and I feel certain something will happen soon in his department."

Up until the very outbreak of war, Lloyd George had believed it could be avoided. However, when faced with the reality, he proved to be the leader with the energy and resolution needed to fight the enemy. The immediate battleground was at home. He had to mobilize industry to new levels of productivity in order to provide, however belatedly, the tools of war.

He turned for help to the men who knew the most about engineering and production. His department was largely staffed by successful businessmen — captains of industry who knew how to run things — and he succeeded in making them into a team. He made a tour of the great engineering centers of Lancashire, the Midlands, and South Wales, meeting with employers and trade-union leaders and appealing from public platforms for the full support of labor. "Plant the flag on your workshops!" he said. "Every lathe you have, recruit it! Convert your machinery into battalions . . . and liberty will be once more enthroned in Europe!" He asked for extra effort on every front and pointed out that discipline was needed just as much at home as it was at the front.

Industry, however, faced an unforeseen difficulty. Because the government had not imposed conscription, or compulsory military service, thousands of skilled workers had volunteered. Lloyd George began to favor conscription, which would allow him to keep the skilled workers home. The Labour movement in Parliament and the trade (labor) unions were strongly opposed to conscription. When Lloyd George went to speak to groups of workers and trade unionists, he was met with hostility.

Conscription remained unpopular, but a convincing argument was found to resolve the unrest at home. Representative workmen were sent to the trenches in Flanders to see what war conditions were like for their countrymen. This helped to ease dissatisfaction at home, and in May 1916 general military service became compulsory.

Another problem that had to be faced was the question of Ireland. A nationalist movement known as *Sinn Fein* ("Ourselves Alone") had established itself in Ireland. In the spring of 1916 the British government learned of a Sinn Fein plot for an Irish uprising and arrested most of the movement's leaders. However, a minority succeeded in launching the Easter Rebellion, which shook Dublin for a week as some 3,000 armed rebels fought the authorities. When the leaders were shot by a firing squad, popular support for Sinn Fein soared.

Lloyd George was chosen by the prime minister, who feared renewed civil violence in Ireland, to negotiate a peaceful solution. He proposed a compromise until after the war and suggested that an empire conference be held then to decide the future relationship of all empire lands. His proposed compromise was thwarted by the House of Lords. The "time of troubles" in Ireland began, and it would be six years before Lloyd George would be in a position to find a solution.

Volunteers line up to enlist at **Southwark Town Hall, 1915.** Britain's lack of a draft policy resulted in the loss of thousands of skilled workers who were desperately needed to run wartime industry.

Workers protest conscription, 1915. To prevent the loss of skilled labor, Lloyd George instituted conscription, or compulsory military service. Trade unions and the Labour party vigorously opposed the policy.

In May 1916, through an error on the German side, the two largest fleets in the world found themselves confronting each other unexpectedly in the North Sea. The Battle of Jutland — the largest naval battle in history — cost the British navy more ships than the Germans, but the British tenaciously held out. Their surface domination of the seas remained virtually unchallenged for the rest of the war.

Although the German fleet ceased to be a danger, its submarines became an ever greater peril. In an attempt to cut off all supplies from Britain, the Germans had decided early in the war to follow a policy of unrestricted submarine warfare, sinking military and nonmilitary vessels alike. In May 1915 the destruction of the *Lusitania* off the coast of Ireland, with a loss of nearly 2,000 lives (over 100 of which were American), had brought angry calls for U.S. entry into the war. By the end of 1916 Germany had increased the number of its submarines, called U-boats, and stepped up the sinking of ships. In June 1916 the British suffered another loss when Kitchener was drowned at sea when the ship he was on struck a mine.

The prime minister had previously divided the functions of the War Office between the secretary of state for war and the chief of the Imperial General Staff (C.I.G.S.), General William Robertson. Kitchener had agreed to this division only because he worked well with Robertson. It would not be easy to find a replacement who would agree to this arrangement. When Asquith offered Lloyd George the position of secretary of state for war, he accepted, even though he was aware of the difficulties of a divided War Office.

Buildings in Dublin show the damage caused by the 1916 Easter Rebellion led by the nationalist *Sinn Fein* party. Lloyd George proposed a truce with the rebels for the duration of the war.

The *Lusitania* docks at New York, 1907. More than 100 Americans were among the 3,000 passengers killed when the ship was sunk by a German submarine in May 1915. An enraged public clamored for U.S. entry into the war against Germany.

The summer of 1916 brought fresh disaster. The Battle of the Somme, a costly British offensive designed to relieve enemy pressure on the French sector of the line, was completely indecisive. By now, 400,000 British lives had been lost. Lloyd George became more and more convinced that the government needed a different method for dealing with the war. Cabinet meetings seemed like debating society contests at a time when firm and decisive action was badly needed. He proposed the formation of a

four-man war cabinet, with himself in charge.

Lloyd George was not the only person who felt that there was a need for change in government. Lack of confidence in Asquith's qualities as a wartime leader led Bonar Law's secretary, Sir Max Aitken (later Lord Beaverbrook), to negotiate a change in leadership. He made a number of delicate inquiries among the Liberal and Conservative leadership, proposing a new coalition.

Asquith rejected Lloyd George's proposal for a war cabinet, and both men resigned. When Asquith sought to form a new government, he was unable to reform his coalition. The king then called on Bonar Law to form a government. He declined, advising the king to send instead for Lloyd George.

A German U-boat halts a neutral Spanish steamship in 1917. In an effort to starve Britain into submission, the Germans focused on unrestricted submarine warfare to cut off all supplies going to and from the island.

6

The Man Who Won the War

To say the circumstances in which Lloyd George became prime minister were peculiar would be an understatement. The manner and consequences of his elevation had far-reaching effects for the Liberal party. Most of the Liberal ministers from the Asquith government and their followers formed a group known as the Independent Liberal party and refused to join Lloyd George's government. The Liberal party never regained its unity.

Lloyd George's opponents doubted that he would be able to form a government, but he confounded his critics and was able to do so by forming a cabinet that was predominantly Conservative. The Conservative party leader, Bonar Law, became chancellor of the Exchequer.

The main feature of Lloyd George's government was the war cabinet that he had proposed to Asquith. It was composed of four ministers who were freed from other duties to devote their full time to running the war. When Labour members accused Lloyd George of appointing four dictators, he re-

He won the greatest war in history. That really was something of an accomplishment.
—LORD BALFOUR
British statesman

A "doughboy" — a U.S. infantryman — awaits his orders in France. When Lloyd George became prime minister in December 1916 the war-weary British were battered and demoralized. Lloyd George enthusiastically welcomed the U.S. entry into the war in April 1917, convinced that the Allies could now quickly end the conflict.

The Imperial War Cabinet sits for a portrait outside 10 Downing Street, the prime minister's residence. Lloyd George (seated fourth from right) created the cabinet, which included representatives from the dominions of the British Empire, to supplement the commanding war cabinet.

plied, "What is a Government for except to dictate? If it does not dictate then it is not a Government, and whether it is four or twenty-three the only difference is that four would take less time than twenty-three."

In forming his government, Lloyd George had to make certain concessions to the Conservative members that would later come to plague him. He was committed to retaining Field Marshal Sir Douglas Haig as commander in chief in France, and he was not to invite Churchill or Alfred Harmsworth (Lord Northcliffe) to join the government. Northcliffe, a journalist, had exposed Kitchener's uncooperativeness by reporting the real conditions of the British soldiers in the trenches.

In December 1916, the very month that Lloyd George took office, the Germans sent a letter to the U.S. government, as an intermediary (the United States had not yet entered the war), expressing Germany's sincere desire for peace. Because Germany immediately released the news of its offer to the international press, the proposal appeared to be a diplomatic endeavor designed to persuade the German public that it was Germany's enemies who desired war. The Allies' reply to Germany stated that they were still awaiting specific proposals and included demands for the restoration and compensation of Belgium, Serbia, and Montenegro and the evacuation (with due reparation) of France, Russia, and Romania.

U.S. president Woodrow Wilson had answered the German letter in good faith. After a long delay the Germans replied to Wilson, making a number of claims and demands betraying the fact that the peace offer had never been seriously intended. The reply also affirmed Germany's intention to continue unrestricted submarine warfare on any ship bound to or from Allied ports. To check the U-boats, Lloyd George revived an old strategy: merchant ships would travel in convoys with a naval escort. This policy was at first opposed by the Admiralty, but Lloyd George prevailed. More ships were built, and merchantmen were armed.

To encourage agricultural self-sufficiency, Lloyd George instituted policies that guaranteed prices for wheat, oats, and potatoes; a minimum farm wage; farm rent control; and compulsory cultivation of land. Parklands and ornamental gardens were to go under the plough; every inch of land was to be cultivated.

Wasteland at Harrow, England, goes under the plow, 1917. With the success of the German U-boat campaign Britain's food shortage reached a critical level, and Lloyd George enacted legislation ordering that all available land be cultivated.

Producing more food was not enough. Shortages still occurred. After an appeal for voluntary restraint did not work, rationing was introduced. The system was a fair one, affecting rich and poor equally. It also helped to slow rising prices. R. E. Prothero, the minister of agriculture, sent Lloyd George an ode that captured the tribulations of rationing:

My Tuesdays are meatless;
My Wednesdays are wheatless;
I'm growing more eatless each day.
My home it is heatless;
My bed it is sheetless—
All are gone to the Y.M.C.A.

The Bar rooms are treatless;
My coffee is sweetless;
Each day I get poorer and wiser.
My socks are now feetless;
My trousers are seatless;
My God! how I do hate the Kaiser.

In the initial years of World War I, U.S. president Woodrow Wilson maintained U.S. neutrality. When German U-boat attacks against American merchant vessels increased, Wilson declared war on Germany.

Early in 1917 Lloyd George sent an invitation to the prime ministers of the British Empire dominions to take part in an Imperial War Cabinet. These countries had already sent a million men to aid the Allies. It seemed more than just to call them together for their views. To the people of Britain, whose morale was often low, the presence of these leaders of the empire was heartening. At this point the entire country had been mobilized for the war effort, but the war was still to be won. The stalemate continued on the western front, and other strategies had failed. It was not yet clear how victory would be achieved.

The answer lay across the Atlantic. Neither the American people nor their president had desired any part in the war: "Peace without Victory" was Woodrow Wilson's theme. But when Germany expanded its submarine warfare, the president appeared before Congress and announced that he had broken off diplomatic relations with Germany. He warned Germany of the consequences if American ships and lives were sacrificed. In reply, the Germans sank the American vessel the *Housatonic* and then the *Lyman M. Law*. From then on, American merchantmen were armed. It finally became impossible to remain neutral.

On April 6, 1917, the United States declared war on Germany. "The world must be made safe for democracy" were Wilson's famous words. Lloyd George had been hoping and waiting for this moment. He immediately sent a special British war mission, led by the foreign secretary, to the United States, where it was given an overwhelmingly enthusiastic welcome. The Allies now had a fresh and unbloodied power on their side. The strength of the United States more than offset what would otherwise have been a calamity: Russia's withdrawal from the war.

The Russians had suffered more than 6 million casualties. Their soldiers were underfed, ragged, often unarmed, and had to face terrible weather conditions, but they had fought bravely for two and a half years. By 1917 conditions on the Russian front were at their worst, and morale was low. In March 1917 a revolution overthrew the Russian tsar, and in November the Bolshevik party assumed power. Dedicated communists, the Bolsheviks regarded the European conflict as a capitalist, imperialist war and signed a separate peace with Germany in March 1918. With Russia in the war, German troops had been diverted from the western front. Now the full strength of the enemy could be brought to bear on the Allies.

Russian princes captured by the German army in East Prussia. In a serious blow to the Allied cause, the Bolsheviks, who had seized power the previous November, signed a peace treaty with Germany in March 1918, releasing German troops on the eastern front.

British flier R. Wentworth Knight ("Tobs") stands in leather gear in front of his plane. World War I saw the first use of air warfare. In response to German air raids, Britain created its Independent Air Force in 1918.

Lloyd George suggested a plan for a sudden attack on the Italian front. Heavy guns and troops could be maneuvered to advance from an unexpected quarter. Both General Robertson and the Italian commander in chief opposed the idea, favoring instead renewed efforts on the western front. Nevertheless, Lloyd George developed a plan for speeding reinforcements to the Italian front. A vast network of railways, built for supplying the troops behind the lines, would have made the maneuver possible via the Julian Alps in Yugoslavia. Rejected at the time, the plan would later play an important part in the war.

Lloyd George was also concerned with the need for unity among the Allied generals. It was an enormous advantage to the Germans that they had a single army and a single command. The generals resisted, but the war cabinet approved a plan to make one Allied army commander temporarily superior to another. Impressed by recent French successes, Lloyd George made British commanders subordinate to General Robert G. Nivelle of the French army.

General Nivelle's offensive was doomed from the start. In April 1917 he launched an attack along a 50-mile front on the Aisne River in France's Champagne region. Five days before the attack the Germans had captured a French soldier who carried the order of battle for all French troops. The enemy knew every movement, and the assault was a disaster. French casualties were more than 100,000, and many thousands more mutinied. Nivelle was relieved of his command by General Henri Pétain, who regained contol of the army.

Nivelle's plan for the western front having failed, Lloyd George turned to Sir Douglas Haig. Haig, however, never revealed to his own government the fact that the main attack would be in Flanders, near the French border in southwest Belgium, and concealed the fact that the French commanders opposed his plan. Indeed, the terrain for the offensive at Ypres could not have been worse. The British troops were to advance over a reclaimed marsh with an elaborate drainage system that would be blown apart by the barrage of gunfire, making the ground a muddy swamp. The biggest mistake Lloyd George made was to allow Haig to proceed, but he had been deceived all along. Haig had even declared that he would not enter upon "a tremendous offensive involving heavy losses."

In spite of predictions of rain, the Battle of Ypres began on July 31. The rain and the ruined drainage system turned the terrain to mud. The casualties were enormous; at the end of the three-month campaign the line had advanced five miles at the cost of some 400,000 lives.

While Haig's leadership was costing his country so dearly, the Germans had been able to divert 10 divisions from the western front to Caporetto, in Slovenia. (Caporetto is now called Kobarid; Slovenia is part of Yugoslavia.) On October 24, German and Austrian troops routed the Italians, penetrating 70 miles beyond the Italian front and killing and capturing over 300,000 of their soldiers. Lloyd George immediately ordered Robertson to put into operation the plan for shifting reinforcements from France and Flanders to the Italian front, which saved the Italian army. On the heels of the crisis in Italy came the Battle of Cambrai in northern France. Haig brought in his tanks, which had been useless in the mud at Ypres. Although the tanks broke through the German lines, the infantry troops were too far behind to support them, and the attack failed.

Lloyd George appointed Sir Douglas Haig Allied commander in 1917. When Haig deliberately withheld information, leading to disastrous losses at Ypres and Cambrai, Lloyd George reorganized the command structure into the new, unified Supreme War Council.

General Ferdinand Foch was the French military representative to the Supreme War Council. In April 1918 he assumed overall command of the Allied armies, including the U.S. troops.

After the twin disasters at Ypres and Caporetto, Lloyd George was determined to shake up the military organization. It seemed more important than ever to unite the Allies under one command. The prime minister had in mind an inter-Allied general staff. At a meeting at Rapallo, Italy, with the French and Italians, a Supreme War Council was set up with a permanent military representative of each country — General Ferdinand Foch for France, Sir Henry Wilson for Britain, and Field Marshal Luigi Cadorna for Italy.

In July 1917 Lloyd George had made a singularly brave decision. As prime minister he always had the loyal support of Bonar Law, the chancellor of the Exchequer. Different as they were, these two men had forged an effective partnership. Now Lloyd George wanted to make a controversial appointment: he wanted Winston Churchill at his side. However, Churchill was enormously unpopular, mainly because of the Dardanelles disaster. Lloyd George thought of giving him a minor appointment, but Churchill would not accept anything but open recognition. It was a difficult position for the prime minister to be in, but he decided to appoint Churchill minister of munitions. Bonar Law, although initially angered by the appointment, helped bring his Conservative colleagues and followers into line. Hostility and jealousy were evident on all sides as a storm of protest erupted. Lloyd George stood by his decision, and Churchill's support would later prove vital.

In March 1918 the Germans launched what was to prove to be their final offensive. The French retreated toward Amiens in order to protect Paris. The British either had to retreat with the French, leaving their channel ports unprotected, or face the threat of a breakthrough in the line dividing the two armies. It was this threat that finally compelled the Allies to entrust the strategic command of the war to General Foch. At this point in the crisis, Lloyd George sent Churchill to France as his personal deputy.

Now that important steps toward coordination had been taken, Lloyd George addressed the over-

whelming problem of manpower. In Britain a new Military Service Bill was passed. This conscription act, designed to ensure that essential reserves were available, made every man between 18 and 50 liable for military service.

At this final hour, the greatest contribution was made by the United States. Lloyd George wrote to Wilson, "It rests with America to win or lose the decisive battles of the war." Wilson sent a mission to London headed by Colonel House, who was invited to discuss plans with the War Cabinet. U.S. troops already in France would be brought into the lines and, like the other Allied troops, would serve under the French commander in chief. Meanwhile, Britain would sacrifice all food imports in order to bring over more desperately needed American troops. Soon more divisions were on their way; in the next three months more than 600,000 American troops crossed the Atlantic.

Parisians celebrate the signing of the armistice on November 11, 1918. Military setbacks and a serious naval mutiny in Germany led Kaiser Wilhelm II to abdicate and flee to Holland.

In May and June the Germans made small advances. By midsummer they had reached the Marne River, where they were held. However, from this point Paris was within range of their long-distance gun, "Big Bertha." On August 8, at Amiens, the British finally used their tanks successfully and shattered the German front. Although victory was ensured, it would take seven more battles to win the German surrender.

Not until October 4, 1918, did the German imperial chancellor ask for an armistice. The war effort had taken a terrible toll in Germany. In early November a naval mutiny began in the ports and spread inland. The kaiser abdicated on November

9 and fled with the crown prince to Holland. On November 11, at 5:00 A.M., the armistice was signed in a railway carriage in Compiègne, France, effective at 11:00 that morning.

At precisely 11:00 A.M. in London sirens screamed and guns thundered. In the streets people sang and danced in the rain. When Lloyd George entered the House of Commons, all the members rose to their feet. He read out the terms of the armistice and then said, "This is no time for words. Our hearts are too full of gratitude, to which no tongue can give adequate expression." The members of the House of Commons then walked in solemn procession across the street to Westminster Abbey.

7

The Years After

However exhilarating the moment of victory had been, peace brought with it new problems. First among these was the overwhelming need to restore stability in Europe. Domestically, Britain had to deal with economic reconstruction. The resources of the nation had been depleted in every way. There also remained the Irish question, which had been deferred for the duration of the war but needed to be solved before civil war broke out there.

It was necessary to call a general election. The members of the House of Commons had been sitting for eight years. As a result of the wartime coalition, the conservatives under Bonar Law continued to support Lloyd George. The Liberals, however, were split — half of Lloyd George's own party remained loyal to former prime minister Asquith. The Labour party, which advocated nationalization of key industries in the interests of the welfare of the workers, had grown and now had a candidate in most constituencies.

The outcome of the election was an overwhelming triumph for the Lloyd George coalition. With the support of the country behind him, his first action was to set out for the Paris peace conference in Versailles, France.

Lloyd George's career was a decisive catalyst in the transition from Victorian Britain to the new society of the 20th century.
—KENNETH O. MORGAN
British historian

At a London garden party Lloyd George earnestly converses with Sir Rufus Isaacs, Lord Reading, who had been involved with him in the 1912 Marconi scandal. Skillfully manipulated by the opposition, reports of shady financial deals and charges of misuse of political funds helped ensure Lloyd George's postwar fall from power.

The 1919 Paris peace conference held at Versailles was dominated by the "Big Four" (seated, left to right): Vittorio Orlando of Italy, Lloyd George, Georges Clemenceau of France, and Wilson. Fearing the dire consequences of the economic ruination of Germany, Lloyd George urged moderation at the talks.

The conference met in January 1919 to determine the terms of Germany's surrender. Representatives from most of the European countries and the United States attended. The three major victorious powers — Britain, France, and the United States — were in a position to make the major decisions. Italy, although one of the victors, had not played quite the same role in the war and did not have the same power at the conference. There were officials from the British Empire dominions, who had played an important part, and there were representatives of all the small nations in central and eastern Europe that sought autonomy. Soviet Russia was not represented; it considered the war a conflict between capitalist nations with problems that did not now apply to Russia.

The three major powers differed profoundly on the terms of the peace because they had been affected by the war to different degrees. France had without doubt suffered more than any other nation. The conflict on French soil had destroyed the land itself. The French casualties far outnumbered those of other victorious nations, and France had known the humiliation and anger of an occupied country. France wanted only one thing: a guarantee that Germany would never again have the power to invade French territory.

Woodrow Wilson came to the conference with a totally different perspective. The United States had not experienced invasion, and its losses were relatively small. Wilson was willing to assist in the construction of a new and better Europe but not become entangled in a permanent alliance.

Britain's position lay somewhere between the two. The country had achieved some of its objectives by the time of the peace conference. Lloyd George also had the support of his country in the desire to grant independence to small nations such as Poland, Czechoslovakia, Serbia, and Romania.

Lloyd George soon realized, however, that Germany would never be able to pay the enormous reparations (payments for damage inflicted) that were being popularly demanded in France and Britain. As a result of the war, Germany already had massive debts. The country would only be destroyed as a result of such heavy demands. The war debt was, in fact, never paid.

The Treaty of Versailles, signed on June 28, 1919, imposed harsh terms on Germany, which was forced to accept responsibility for the war. Germany lost territory to France and Belgium, was stripped of its overseas colonies, and was obliged to drastically reduce its military. On the bitterly debated question of reparations Lloyd George tried to bring the Allies to a compromise and propose a realistic sum, but he found himself outvoted. He was then criticized when he returned to London for not having gained enough in reparations.

Nevertheless, some balance of power had been restored to Europe, and an era of peace seemed a reasonable hope. Wilson's League of Nations, a forum for discussion of international issues, had been established as a means to that end. Lloyd George now turned his attention to Britain's concerns at home. An immediate problem was Ireland.

At the beginning of the war the Irish nationalists had declared a moratorium on their own struggles in order to support Britain in a time of peril. The Irish Republic, which had suffered a setback during the Easter Rebellion in 1916, was proclaimed again in Dublin in 1918. In January, 26 of the Sinn Fein

British soldiers warily watch the streets of Dublin, 1920. When violence erupted following the 1918 proclamation of an independent Irish republic, British troops were sent in to restore order.

Eamon De Valera was the leader of Sinn Fein. When Lloyd George reached an agreement with Irish leaders in 1921 to partition Ireland and create the Irish Free State as a self-governing dominion, De Valera denounced the treaty and refused to participate in the new Irish government.

members elected in December 1918 refused to take their seats in Parliament. They set up an assembly in Dublin that declared Irish independence. Soon, violence became the order of the day as the Irish Republican Army, the military wing of Sinn Fein, targeted hostile forces in Ireland, including members of the Irish police force, which was controlled by England. The English responded with an army of occupation that numbered 43,000 by autumn.

Lloyd George believed that a relatively small gang was making it impossible for reasonable men to come together and reach an agreement. He continued to believe that order could be restored to Ireland, but he could not allow Sinn Fein to form a republic. First of all, Ulster would never submit. Second, he stood at the head of a coalition that was predominantly Conservative and would not agree to independence. Beyond that, he was answerable to the British public. Home Rule, with continued ties to Great Britain, remained his policy.

King George was to go to Belfast in June 1921 to open the first session of the new Ulster Parliament. Realizing that the occasion provided an unusual opportunity, Lloyd George wrote a speech for the king in which he stressed the importance of Ireland in the eyes of the rest of the empire and the fact that the empire represented diverse nations and races that chose to remain tied together in spite of ancient feuds. He appealed "to all Irishmen to pause, to stretch out the hand of forbearance and conciliation, to forgive and forget, and to join in making for the land they love a new era of peace, contentment and goodwill."

Having seized this public occasion for a statement of policy, Lloyd George entered into secret and protracted negotiations with the various Sinn Fein leaders, among them Michael Collins and Arthur Griffith. Eamon De Valera, the most important Sinn Fein leader, would not participate. The negotiations were often frustrating, and there were many anxious moments. A treaty was signed on December 6, 1921, that formally divided Ireland. The Catholic south became the Irish Free State, a self-governed dominion within the British Empire. De Valera and other members of Sinn Fein refused to recognize the treaty or the partition, and the violent strife within Ireland continued.

For Lloyd George, however, the end of his days as prime minister were at hand. Despite his appointment of a ministry of reconstruction to give special attention to issues raised in postwar Britain, the problems caused by the demobilization of millions of war veterans and the difficulties in changing from a wartime to a peacetime economy were often overwhelming.

The reconstruction proposals that had been framed had assumed more continuity in economic conditions than actually prevailed. The returning soldiers had been promised that the government would "make Britain a fit country for heroes to live in." An unprecedented economic boom ensued, with companies filling orders and pouring money into expansion. This in turn led to inflation, and trade unions were concerned with keeping wages in line with rising costs. There were more strikes in the postwar period than at any other time in Britain's history. A slump and unemployment followed; 2 million workers were out of a job. The coalition government, weakened by the resolution of the Irish problem, which many Conservatives considered a

Armed guards of the Irish Free State patrol in January 1922. A civil war was fought in Ireland over the establishment of the free state. In England, opposition within Lloyd George's coalition government to his Irish solution helped bring about the government's downfall.

sellout, lost even more support because of the economic slump.

While the leaders of the Conservative party continued to support the coalition, many backbenchers wanted an independent Conservative party. Finally, Bonar Law himself decided to stand with the dissident backbenchers and asked the king to dissolve Parliament and call for a general election on November 15, 1922. The Conservative party went to the polls on a platform that stressed "tranquility and freedom from adventures and commitments both at home and abroad." At the polls, the party and its policy won a substantial victory. Labour had also gained enormously, winning more votes than the Liberal party, which was now split between the Asquith and Lloyd George supporters.

The manner in which Lloyd George, then 59, left office was characteristic. He did so quite cheerfully, without the slightest drama. He did not return to obscurity, however. He held his seat in the Commons until 1944, at which time he had done so continuously for 54 years.

One of the first things Lloyd George did after leaving office was to undertake a journey to the United States and Canada in the summer of 1923. His welcome when he arrived in New York charmed and delighted him. A fleet of boats escorted his ship into the harbor while a squadron of aircraft dipped in salute overhead. Newspaper reporters and photographers swarmed on board. He could not have been given a warmer greeting, and with his natural charm he responded with praise for the country that had come to Britain's aid. Wherever he went on his speaking tour, he was met by the same enthusiastic crowds — 400,000 turned out to hear him address an outdoor meeting in Cleveland. He returned home in the fall.

He had built a house (called "Bron-y-de," or "slope of the south") at Churt in Surrey, about 45 miles from London, where he spent most of his time. When he left office he took with him all his records. Based on these, he composed his *War Memoirs* and two subsequent volumes on the Paris peace conference. He continued to develop his ideas in a series of published reports on coal and power, trade, industry, agriculture, and transport. Lloyd George still expected to be returned to office but was disappointed in the hope. Although there was more than one reason for his political eclipse, there is no doubt that one question in particular did him and his party great harm.

In 1922 questions had been asked in the Commons on the government's practice of bestowing "honors" — that is, in recommending that the king elevate certain businessmen to one of the five ranks of British nobility. It was even charged that honors had been awarded in return for monetary contributions. Lloyd George's defense at the time was that he had done nothing in the way of awarding honors that was any different from the practice of past ministries. It was impossible to establish whether or not money had passed hands.

One incontrovertible fact remained. During the period of his coalition government, Lloyd George had established a political treasure chest, initially named the "National Liberal Party Political Fund," which was supposed to have collected between £1 and £2 million in just four years. It was widely assumed that Lloyd George had bestowed "honors" in return for contributions. The truth of the matter is obscure, but Lloyd George maintained that the fund existed because of his own hard work and exertions and that it was a trust for his own use in political causes of his choice.

Whatever the facts of the case, the whole matter bred scandal and suspicion. As a cause of dissension, it resulted in great damage to the Liberal party. Above all, it did irreparable harm to Lloyd George's great name. It was undoubtedly a tragedy that such a question should have marred his later years.

In 1929 the Liberal party, with Lloyd George at its head, suffered a terrible defeat at the polls. The loss was a bitter disappointment, but he could, however, take comfort in the fact that two of his children had been returned to the House of Commons — his son Gwilym from Pembroke and daughter Megan for Anglesey. He himself introduced Megan when she took her seat in the Commons.

In October 1943, two years after the death of his wife, Lloyd George married his longtime secretary and mistress, Frances Stevenson. Ill with cancer and depressed by his country's handling of World War II, he spent his last years reminiscing about Wales.

Britain found itself again on the verge of war in 1939. After some initial indifference to the aggressive moves of Hitler, Lloyd George bitterly reproached the British government for its weakness and vacillation in the prewar years. After war had been declared, he remained critical of the country's leadership. In May 1940, when Winston Churchill was summoned to lead the country, he in his turn wanted to have Lloyd George in his cabinet, but Lloyd George was now 77, and he turned down Churchill's offer. It was not only that he felt the demands of office were beyond his powers; he did not believe in the way the war cabinet was constituted. There were desperate times ahead, and Lloyd George, listening to the radio in Churt, heard only the endless account of defeat and disaster.

Early in 1941 news reached him that his wife was seriously ill. At once he departed for Criccieth, but the terrible winter storm that was blowing across the land prevented him from reaching her in time. He did not reach Criccieth until the day after she died. He was utterly heartbroken.

After Margaret's death, he returned to the house in Churt, but his appearances in the House of Commons became increasingly rare. He was depressed, and he was also critical of the government's handling of the war. His feelings created a sharp disagreement with his old friend Churchill, who even at that stage wanted to make use of Lloyd George's experience and advice.

In October 1943 he and his secretary, Frances Stevenson, were married after an association of more than 30 years. At first they kept their marriage a secret, but when they announced it they received the warmest congratulations from all sides. He needed her more than ever now, for soon after their marriage his doctors diagnosed cancer. At the end of his life, he began to think more and more about his boyhood in Wales. Often he would talk to Frances about Criccieth and of returning there.

On June 6, 1944 — D-day — he and Frances heard the news on the radio that Allied forces had invaded Normandy in northern France. They drove to London, where Lloyd George rushed to the House of Commons to offer warm congratulations to Churchill. Soon afterward, he and Frances left for Llanystumdwy.

Looming over him was the thought of the next election. He knew that he could not fight it. When Churchill offered him an earldom, he accepted it as a way of remaining in Parliament. Lloyd George's life was full of anomalies, not the least of which was that he should finally end it as a member of the House of Lords, which he had so vehemently attacked in his younger days.

On March 26, 1945, with Frances and Megan on either side of his bed, he died. He was buried in his favorite glade, his body carried on a farm wagon covered in flowers and spring leaves, in his beloved Wales.

> *As a man of action, resource and creative energy he stood, when at his zenith, without a rival. Much of his work abides, some of it will grow greatly in the future, and those who come after us will find the pillars of his life's toil upstanding, massive and indestructible.*
> —WINSTON CHURCHILL
> British prime minister

Further Reading

Cross, Colin. *The Liberals in Power 1905–1914*. London: Barrie and Rockliff with Pall Mall Press, 1963

George, William. *My Brother and I.* London: Eyre and Spottiswoode, 1958

George, W. R. P. *The Making of Lloyd George.* Connecticut: The Shoe String Press, 1976

Gilbert, Martin. *Lloyd George.* New Jersey: Prentice-Hall, 1968

Grigg, John. *Lloyd George: The People's Champion 1902–1911.* Berkeley and Los Angeles: University of California Press, 1978

Lloyd-George, Earl. *My Father, Lloyd George.* New York: Crown Publishers, 1961

Mee, Charles L., Jr. *The End of Order—Versailles 1919.* New York: Dutton, 1980

Morgan, Kenneth O. *Lloyd George Family Letters 1885–1936.* London: University of Wales Press, Cardiff and Oxford University Press, 1973

Stokesbury, James L. *A Short History of World War I.* New York: William Morrow and Company, 1981

Chronology

Jan. 17, 1863	Born David George in Manchester, England
1864	William George (father) dies; family moves to Llanystumdwy to live with Richard Lloyd (uncle)
1878–82	Lloyd George apprentices with law firm
1884	Passes Law Society examination
1888	Marries Margaret Owen
1890	Wins the Caernarvon Boroughs Parliament seat for the Liberal party in a bi-election
1892	Is elected to first full term; supports Home Rule for Ireland; agitates for the disestablishment of the Anglican church
1895	Breaks with the Liberal leadership on the disestablishment issue
1905	Liberal party wins general election; Sir Henry Campbell-Bannerman becomes prime minister; Lloyd George named president of the Board of Trade
1908	Campbell-Bannerman resigns and Herbert Asquith succeeds him as prime minister; Lloyd George appointed chancellor of the Exchequer
1914	German forces invade Belgium, drawing Great Britain into World War I commitment
1915	Lloyd George named minister of munitions
1916	After the Easter Rebellion, Lloyd George negotiates a temporary settlement between Irish nationalists and British government
	Military setbacks undermine confidence in Asquith government; Asquith resigns; King George V calls on Lloyd George to form a government
1917	Lloyd George establishes war cabinet
Nov. 11, 1918	Germany surrenders, ending World War I
Dec. 1918	General election confirms Lloyd George's coalition government
1919	Lloyd George represents Britain at the Paris peace conference and signs the Treaty of Versailles
	Irish republic proclaimed; British forces occupy Ireland
1921	Lloyd George signs treaty securing "dominion" status for the Republic of Ireland
1922	Resigns as prime minister
1929–44	Serves as a member of the House of Commons
1940	Refuses a seat in the cabinet of Prime Minister Winston Churchill
1941	Margaret Lloyd George dies
1943	Lloyd George marries Frances Stevenson
1944	Accepts the earldom of Dwyfor
March 26, 1945	David Lloyd George dies in Wales

Index

Deirdre Shearman was born in the British Isles and educated in England, Switzerland, and the United States, where she has lived since 1959. She is the mother of three sons. Her principal historical interest is the British raj in India. She is also the author of *Queen Victoria* in the Chelsea House series WORLD LEADERS PAST & PRESENT.

Arthur M. Schlesinger, jr., taught history at Harvard for many years and is currently Albert Schweitzer Professor of the Humanities at City University of New York. He is the author of numerous highly praised works in American history and has twice been awarded the Pulitzer Prize. He served in the White House as special assistant to Presidents Kennedy and Johnson.

PICTURE CREDITS

AP/Wide World Photos: p. 106; The Bettmann Archive: pp. 2, 18, 26, 35, 38, 40, 43, 44, 45, 50, 57, 66, 69, 74, 75, 79, 82, 86, 88, 90, 91, 93, 95, 98, 100, 101, 102; The Bettmann Archive/BBC Hulton: pp. 14, 21, 24, 25, 31, 36, 54–55, 58, 64, 70, 81, 83, 89, 103; British Information Service: p. 52; Courtesy of the author: p. 92; Courtesy of W. R. P. George: pp. 15, 16, 19, 22, 23; Culver Pictures: pp. 28, 29, 30, 33, 46–47, 60, 63, 72, 76, 78, 80, 84, 85, 94; Press Association, London: pp. 32, 49; Barry Simon: p. 77; UPI/Bettmann Newsphotos: pp. 96–97